Learning Thai, Your Great Adventure

by Russ Crowley & Duangta Wanthong Mondi

Published by Russ Crowley

Front cover and all illustrations by Toni Howard.
Tone graph created and drawn by Russ Crowley.
All photographs by Russ Crowley.
Translated by Duangta Wanthong Mondi.

Read What Others Have Said About Quest

I have achieved more than I would have thought possible in such a short space of time. Your colour code and picture aids make learning so much easier and it's so easy to refresh my memory from your app. I must say Russ, for me your product has been a great help, well worth the small price paid, and, would wholeheartedly recommend it to anyone wanting to learn to read and write Thai.

Orville Earle, London, UK, 17th October 2013

Your teaching technique is very good, much better than the other books I've seen.

Julian Wheeler, Chonburi, Thailand, 28th October 2012

The Thai language is very intimidating and this program has taken the fear away! I would give it an 11 out of 10 points!! Thanks Russ!

Sandra Ching, Ecuador, 9th September 2013

I agree that your app and those posts are like a speed-of-light catalyst in terms teaching one the Thai script and reading it within literally two days (in my experience) which I find extraordinary!... I am just extremely excited that I have finally found material that does not throw one into the deep end of things.

Emiliusz Smorczewski, Illinois, USA, 9th July 2013

I have been very pleased with how quickly I have been able to learn and retain so much. Another aspect to purchasing is the quality of service received. The iPad version is awesome because I can use it anywhere without internet. I travel a lot and often am without internet, so it makes it nice.

Brian Atwell, USA, 3rd October 2013

Your book made learning the pronunciation and alphabet very easy. Thanks again.

Allen Mitchell, 9th April 2013

This is the best help I've had, thank you so much, really easy to understand.

Rebekah Wilkes, UK, 7th May 2013

I'm surprised at how quickly and easily this is all sinking in. Thanks for making it easy.

Mitch Costello, Sydney, Australia, 9th September 2013

These resources are making the learning of Thai a reality after numerous false starts... the simplicity of the system breaks down the psychological barriers to attacking the idea of reading/writing Thai.

Brock Estes, Richmond, VA, 15th September 2012

Our Other Quest Products

We currently have 4 books and 2 applications with Quest:

- Volume 1 - *Learning Thai, Your Great Adventure*
- Volume 2 - *Learn Thai Alphabet with Memory Aids to Your Great Adventure*
- Volume 3 - *The Perfect Thai Phrasebook*
- Volume 4 - *How to Read Thai*

The Learn Thai Alphabet application is a web-based (pc or Mac) and iPad application to teach you the Thai alphabet. Based on our 2nd book (vol 2) the app offers interaction, quizzes, sounds by native speakers and much more.

The Learn Thai Numbers application runs on the same systems and gets you up to speed with the Thai numbers system in record time - a must have if you want to excel with, and complete your Thai studies.

Check out our website for details: **www.learnthaialphabet.com**

For Joan and Bill Crowley, mum & dad.

Table of Contents

Learning Thai, Your Great Adventure

Quest - Quick, Easy, Simple Thai

Welcome to *Quest*, our system for learning Thai. Whether you have any other materials for learning Thai: books, audio, web pages, etc., we are positive that *Learning Thai, Your Great Adventure* and our system as a whole, will surprise you in more ways than one.

Whatever your language goals, we provide you with enough to take you to where you want to be. According to the Foreign Services Institute (Effective Language Learning, 2013), Thai is in category IV of the language difficulty ranking (V being the hardest) and requires around 1100 hours of study to reach Speaking 3: General Professional Proficiency in Speaking (S3), and Reading 3: General Professional Proficiency in Reading (R3); so, though it's not as difficult as some languages, as with any studying, it all depends on many factors, including: 1) the target language; 2) the aptitude and ability of the learner; and 3) the material being used.

If you have tried studying with other materials, you will know that it can vary considerably in both quality and complexity. Indeed, Russ tried many different websites, books, etc., while learning Thai and struggled with the inconsistency of other materials; and, without a single, logical, end-to-end system, found he spent a considerable amount of time and effort just trying to get past the basics; and is one of the principal reasons why we came up with our *Quest* system and why it will help you

What is Quest?

Quest stands for *Quick, Easy, Simple Thai* and is the system we've designed to take an absolute beginner through to being able to read Thai. It differs from other material in that the books can be studied independently — they are standalone — or they can be used either in order or as reference material as part of our end-end system.

Who is this Book For

Quest Volume 1 - Learning Thai, Your Great Adventure is targeted at two types of learner: 1) absolute beginners to the Thai language; and, 2) for those learners who have studied or have some knowledge of Thai, but find themselves stuck in a rut with no other place to go.

For the former, you definitely have an advantage as you don't have to unlearn any other systems, and can proceed quickly through learning about the Thai language, the alphabet, tone, and move onto speaking, reading and writing Thai. For the latter, with your existing knowledge, you will just need to familiarise yourself with the consonant and vowel sounds and names we use, the acronyms, the rules, the hints, tips and tricks which make *Quest - Quick, Easy, Simple Thai*. Having said that, it is important

Wat Sothonwararam Worawihan, 'Wat Hong', Chachoengsao Province.

that you don't skip any thing, but you could find that you might not need to dwell on certain parts as much as a beginner does.

As such, LTYGA is, by design, of great use to the first time holiday-maker, to the seasoned traveller, or for anyone who wants to spend more time in the Land of Smiles (LOS), and who also wants to improve their level of Thai. From the novice through to the experienced, this book is for you.

As we said in the first paragraph of this section, LTYGA is targeted at those new to Thai and to our system; and, as it is an introduction to the Thai language and our method of teaching, in itself it won't get you to a high level of Thai — that will require much studying and a book many times this size — but, it will get you started, it will familiarise you with our system, and it will get you well on your way to achieving a basic level of speaking, reading, and writing Thai, quickly and easily.

As **Brock Estes** wrote:

> *"...the simplicity of the system breaks down the psychological barriers to attacking the idea of reading/writing Thai... if you are serious about learning Thai, you will not regret any of the time you spend early on with this material."*

This will then provide a solid platform for continuation of your Thai language studies within our *Quest* system.

How to Use this Book

There is a lot to digest in this book so please don't think you can get through it in one go. We've divided it into 5 main sections: 1) *The Thai Alphabet* — where we introduce the alphabet, the consonants and the vowels; 2) *Speaking Thai* — where we go through grammar and tone; 3) *Reading Thai* — where we cover the 8 rules that are essential to know for reading Thai, plus where to write vowels, silent consonants, and other consonant rules; 4) *Writing Thai* - where we show you how easy it is to learn to write the Thai characters; and, 5) *The Consonant story* - unlike the Roman alphabet, the

Thai alphabet order is difficult to learn. Not only have we constructed a simple story to connect the consonants in order, but we also show you how you can start to read Thai from the earliest stage.

If you want to get started with Thai straight away, then you can either go to the first page of the story (the Chicken, on page 56) and read and learn from the transliterated Thai and the English translation of common sentences, or you can go to Useful Phrases on page 165.

However, if you do wish to learn to speak, read, and write Thai, then the first step is to learn a little about the language, and then about the Thai alphabet.

Wat Phra Sing Waramahawihan, Chiang Mai

Everybody has specific ways they like to learn and it is up to you to determine yours. Whatever method you use, remember that when learning any language, regular sessions are necessary and immersing yourself and practising at any opportunity is the best way to go.

Of course, if you only visit the LOS on holiday then this may be a little more difficult but there is now a wealth of support available on the Internet to help you: websites, podcasts, chat, and so on; but, as we said before, though some of this is questionable, there are always genuine Thai people who would love to converse with you and, as you practice your Thai, they can practice their English.

Naturally, when you combine the information from this book with actually using Thai, your time in Thailand will be further enriched by having made new friends on the way.

1. The Alphabet

There are 44 consonants (อัก-ษร - àk-sɔ̌ɔn[1], *consonant*) in the Thai language and 32 vowels (สี-ระ - sà-rà, *vowel*). Of these, 2 consonants and 2 vowels are no longer used (they're obsolete), and another 4 vowels are extremely rare; but, you will still need to learn them.

When you see written Thai script, you will see that vowels are placed in front of, above, below, and behind consonants. You will also see that there are other 'strange marks' written above the consonants (and often above the vowels that are written above the consonants) as well. We realise that all these are probably brand new to you, but don't worry as all will be explained in due course.

To start though, one of the main differences between the English and Thai is Thai is a tonal language. This means that if you get the tone of a syllable or a word wrong, then there's a possibility that you may be misunderstood. As such, it is important that you try and get the tone correct, otherwise there may be occasions when it may prove difficult to get your message across.

Thai script encompasses everything within the writing system itself to enable you to read, to calculate the correct tone, etc. But until we have got that far, we need something we can use right now - we use what is called transliterated Thai text.

---

1. *Don't worry about how to pronounce this at the moment, all will be revealed soon.*

Transliterated Thai

Transliterated Thai (or transliterated text) is a romanised translation of Thai script which incorporates both syllable breakdown and the correct tone.

If you already know a little Thai, then you're probably aware that there is no agreed transliteration of Thai script, and at last count there were 12 different systems; so, if you already have three or four books on learning Thai then it's quite possible you have an equal number of different transliteration systems.

Ideally, you want to be able to read Thai script, but until that happens, you're stuck with a language system which, to all intents and purposes, is useless to you: only foreigners or Thai language teachers teaching foreigners use transliterated Thai.

In our experience, the most accurate and easiest transliterated system to use is that developed by Paiboon Publishing.

It is a simple to use, comprehensive system that incorporates the information you need to understand and speak Thai. There are a number of benefits to their system, one of which is in the use of a single letter to represent short vowels and a double letter for long vowels (the vowels in the examples in Table 1.1 are all long vowels): it's simple, obvious, and provides an easy-to-see and easy-to-use method of differentiating between similar words. They have kindly granted permission for us to use their Paiboon and Paiboon+ systems and we will be using them throughout our system.

However, and right from the start, we cannot emphasise enough the need to start learning Thai script. Every second you spend learning transliterated Thai is a second of time wasted - Thai script may initially be difficult, but once you have the basics, you'll be so pleased that you did.

Writing Transliterated Tones

There are 5 tones in Thai (high, mid, low, falling and rising) and, when we write transliterated text, we write the tone mark above the first vowel in the word as shown in Table 1.1. The table also shows examples of how the tones are written and how the tone is to be pronounced:

Table 1.1 - Transliterated Thai Tone Marks

Tone	Tone Mark	Transliter-ated Thai Example	You Say it With...
Middle	No tone sign	Gaa	...your normal voice, constant pitch.
Low	\	Gàa	...your voice *starting* at a slightly lower pitch than your normal (mid tone) voice and *dropping* throughout.
Falling	^	Gâa	...your voice *starting* higher than your mid tone, rises briefly, and then drops, *finishing* lower than mid tone.
High	/	Gáa	...your voice *starting* higher than mid tone and *rising* throughout.
Rising	v	Găa	....your voice *starts* slightly lower than mid tone, falls briefly, and then rises, *finishing* higher than mid tone.

Note: The symbols used to identify tone are *only used in transliterated script*. Thai script has its own written tone marks and these are covered in section 5.

Tone Graph

With each tone it is important that you understand the level where the tone starts and finishes. For example, low tone may sound similar to falling tone at first but remember that low tone starts below mid tone and keeps dropping, whereas falling tone starts higher than mid tone and then, after rising briefly, it drops [below your mid tone].

Every Thai student learns the **base** tone sequence for Middle Class conso-nants: *gaa, gàa, gâa, gáa, gǎa - middle, low, falling, high, rising,* respec-tively. This is because only the Middle Class consonants can produce all 5 tones (this will become apparent in section 5).

When they have mastered this they then move onto the base tones for High and Low Class consonants. All other words are then compared against these base tones to ensure correctness.

When learning the language, getting the tone correct can be one of the hardest tasks facing Westerners. However, don't be put off by speaking Thai as most of the time you will be understood by the context anyway; indeed, Kon Tai (Thai people) are very friendly and love to hear foreigners using their language; and, if you ask them, they would love to help you with your pronunciation, new words, and the language. Besides, and at the very least, you could cheer up someone's day - just persevere, it's well worth it. Figure 1.1.1 provides a graphical explanation of tone pitch:

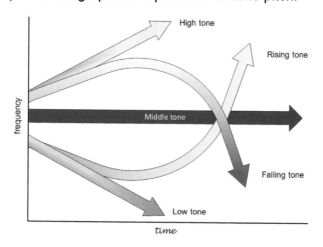

Figure 1.1.1 The 5 Thai Tones

2. Consonants

We mentioned earlier that there are 44 consonants in the Thai alphabet, and one of the difficulties with the Thai alphabet is that there is often more than one consonant character for a particular sound. For example, there are 6 consonants that make the /**k**/ sound: 5 as an initial consonant and 1 as a final consonant; therefore, and to avoid confusion, we need a method to differentiate between consonants.

To do this, every Thai consonant has a name that gives us both the sound the consonant makes and its distinguishing name, this name is comprised of three component parts:

1. The sound that the consonant makes; this is <u>always</u> the first or a combination of the first *and* second letters of the consonant name, e.g. /**g**/, /**k**/, /**ng**/, /**ch**/, etc.

2. An inherent vowel (this appears in every consonant); and

3. a noun that identifies the consonant.

The first consonant of the Thai alphabet is called Gɔɔ Gài. We mentioned the Paiboon Transliteration System in the introduction and the ɔɔ characters we see in the first word help describe the vowel sound that this consonant makes.

This particular sound is like the *aw* in the word *<u>aw</u>ful*. The standard convention for writing this sound is /-/. So, for Gɔɔ Gài, the Gɔɔ part is pronounced /**g**/ +/**aw**/ and combined they are written as /gɔɔ/.

*

You will see some other unfamiliar characters in the List of Consonants and Sounds, Table 2.2.1. These characters and the sounds they make are all explained in Table 3.1.2 (page 19) and Table 3.1.4 (on page 20).

In Thai, Gɔɔ Gài is written as ก ไก่ and it is comprised of:

- ก – the consonant. This consonant makes the 'G' sound (**g** as in 'galahad'. Using the above convention, we write this as /**g**/).

- The 'ɔɔ' part. This is an inherent part of every consonant and transforms the consonant sound into a word. It comes from the consonant ɔɔ Àang (อ อ่าง) (ɔɔ Àang is covered in more detail in section 8.2).

- ไก่ (Gài) – this is the name of the 'item' the consonant refers to.

  Gài means *chicken* and the Thai spelling is comprised of:

  - the vowel ไ-, giving the vowel sound /**ai**/ (as in the 'y' in *fl**y***);

  - the consonant ก, giving the consonant sound /**g**/; and

  - the tone mark ่ (above the ก - covered in section 5).

When we wish to give an example without using a specific consonant, we mark the position of the consonant with a hyphen (-). So, in this example, we can see that the hyphen is **after** the vowel สระ ไ- (sà-rà /**ai**/) which means this vowel is <u>always</u> written before a consonant.

One important note is that regardless of where the vowel is written, the consonant sound is always pronounced first, i.e. ไก is pronounced /**g**/ + /**ai**/ = /**gai**/ <u>not</u> /**ai**/ + /**g**/ = /**aig**/. This is covered in detail in section 7 but please embed and remember this point (the tone mark above ก has been deliberately omitted here).

2.1 Start in the Middle

When learning the Thai alphabet, we being by learning the consonants first. There's little point in learning the vowels until you understand about the alphabet and about the consonants.

The reason for this is, in Thai, consonants and vowels cannot be combined into an easy method such as the Roman alphabets' A, B, C, D, E...; consequently, you must learn the consonants first. The main difference here is that when learning the Thai alphabet, it's not feasible to learn the consonants in the actual A,B,C-type order as we do in English — it just doesn't make sense. What we must do is learn them according to the 'class' they belong to.

As we covered briefly before, Thai is a tonal language and a key component in determining tone is the class the consonant belongs to - the *consonant class*. There are 3 of them: High, Middle, and Low, and every consonant belongs to 1 of these classes (and 1 only, consonants never change class).

We'll come onto the classes and the colours in more detail shortly, but when learning the classes, it makes sense to start with the smallest group — this is the Middle Class group and there are a total of 9 Middle Class consonants.

To learn the consonants, you need to learn their shapes, to recognise and write them; to learn the class they belong to, to calculate tone; and, to learn the sound or sounds that they make, in order to speak it; (later on, you can also learn their proper Thai names, but that's not essential at the start, recognising the shapes and knowing the sound(s) they make is far more important).

In the consonant story, the Middle Class consonants are the ones with the yellow header and footer bars, but we will look at the complete table of consonants next, in the order they appear in the alphabet. The Middle Class consonants are the ones coloured orange (yellow text doesn't show up particularly well on a white page).

2.2 Consonant List

Table 2.2.1 shows the complete list of Thai consonants, their order, transliterated text name, meaning, sound, and the class of the consonant.

Table 2.2.1 - List of Consonants and Sounds

No.	Thai Character	Transliterated Text Name	Meaning	Sound	As In...	Class (H, M, L)
1	ก ไก่	Gɔɔ Gài	Chicken	/g/	galahad	Middle
2	ข ไข่	Kɔ̌ɔ Kài	Egg	/k/	kangaroo	High
3	ฃ ขวด	Kɔ̌ɔ Kùuat	Bottle	/k/	karaoke	High
4	ค ควาย	Kɔɔ Kwaai	Buffalo	/k/	koala	Low
5	ฅ คน	Kɔɔ Kon	Person	/k/	koala	Low
6	ฆ ระฆัง	Kɔɔ Rá-kang	Bell	/k/	kite	Low
7	ง งู	Ngɔɔ Nguu	Snake	/ng/	guarding	Low
8	จ จาน	Jɔɔ Jaan	Plate	/j/	jabberwocky	Middle
9	ฉ ฉิ่ง	Chɔ̌ɔ Chìng	Cymbals	/ch/	chat	High
10	ช ช้าง	Chɔɔ Cháang	Elephant	/ch/	chef	Low
11	ซ โซ่	Sɔɔ Sôo	Chain	/s/	saxophone	Low
12	ฌ เฌอ	Chɔɔ Chəə	Tree	/ch/	child	Low
13	ญ หญิง	Yɔɔ Yíng	Woman	/y/	you	Low
14	ฎ ชฎา	Dɔɔ Chá-daa	Head-dress	/d/	dog	Middle
15	ฏ ปฏัก	Dtɔɔ Bpà-dtàk	Spear	/dt/	dog	Middle
16	ฐ ฐาน	Tɔ̌ɔ Tăan	Pedestal	/t/	tassle	High
17	ฑ มณโฑ	Tɔɔ Mon-too	Giant's Wife	/t/	tortoise	Low
18	ฒ ผู้เฒ่า	Tɔɔ Pûu-tâo	Old Man	/t/	training	Low
19	ณ เณร	Nɔɔ Neen	Monk	/n/	napoleon	Low
20	ด เด็ก	Dɔɔ Dèk	Child	/d/	damsel	Middle

Table 2.2.1 - List of Consonants and Sounds

21	ต เต่า	Dtɔɔ Dtào	Turtle	/dt/	damsel	Middle
22	ถ ถุง	Tɔ̌ɔ Tǔng	Bag	/t/	top	High
23	ท ทหาร	Tɔɔ Tá-hǎan	Soldier	/t/	typist	Low
24	ธ ธง	Tɔɔ Tong	Flag	/t/	tea	Low
25	น หนู	Nɔɔ Nǔu	Mouse	/n/	navigating	Low
26	บ ใบไม้	Bɔ̌ɔ Bai-mái	Leaf	/b/	bald	Middle
27	ป ปลา	Bpɔɔ Bplaa	Fish	/bp/	bottom	Middle
28	ผ ผึ้ง	Pɔ̌ɔ Pʉ̂ng	Bee	/p/	profit	High
29	ฝ ฝา	Fɔ̌ɔ Fǎa	Lid	/f/	fruit	High
30	พ พาน	Pɔɔ Paan	Tray	/p/	pray	Low
31	ฟ ฟัน	Fɔɔ Fan	Tooth	/f/	finish	Low
32	ภ สำเภา	Pɔɔ Sǎm-pao	Junk	/p/	paint	Low
33	ม ม้า	Mɔɔ Máa	Horse	/m/	map	Low
34	ย ยักษ์	Yɔɔ Yák	Giant	/y/	yeti	Low
35	ร เรือ	Rɔɔ Rʉʉa	Boat	/r/	rabbit	Low
36	ล ลิง	Lɔɔ Ling	Monkey	/l/	large	Low
37	ว แหวน	Wɔɔ Wɛ̌ɛn	Ring	/w/	wave	Low
38	ศ ศาลา	Sɔ̌ɔ Sǎa-laa	Tent	/s/	sign	High
39	ษ ฤๅษี	Sɔ̌ɔ Rʉʉ-sǐi	Hermit	/s/	sea	High
40	ส เสือ	Sɔ̌ɔ Sʉ̌ʉa	Tiger	/s/	squirrel	High
41	ห หีบ	Hɔ̌ɔ Hìip	Chest	/h/	humps	High
42	ฬ จุฬา	Lɔɔ Jù-laa	Star-shaped Kite	/l/	look	Low
43	อ อ่าง	ɔɔ Àang	Bowl	/ɔɔ/	awful	Middle
44	ฮ นกฮูก	Hɔɔ Nók-hûuk	Owl	/h/	hooray	Low

As you can see from the table, some sounds are made by more than one consonant; and, to avoid confusion, when referring to a consonant, its full name is always used, e.g. Gɔɔ Gài, Kɔ̌ɔ Kài...

For example, คนจน. There are two words here, คน+จน (Thai script has very few spaces in it). These are pronounced *kon jon* and mean *poor man*: kon = *person*, jon = *poor*. If you had to spell these out, you would spell them, "*kɔɔ kwaai, nɔɔ nǔu, jɔɔ jaan, nɔɔ nǔu*".

At this stage it is unlikely that you would have noticed that all the letters here are consonants; yet, when you pronounce, "*kon jon*", you hear two vowels: an /o/ in both *kon* and *jon:* Thai has both written and unwritten vowels (these will be covered in section 7.2).

Note: a quick note, it may help you to think of the Thai alphabet in the same way we learn the Roman alphabet, e.g. where we think of A, /ei/ Alpha; B, /**bi:**/, Bravo; C, /**ci:**/ Charlie (using the Cambridge phonetic system), try and think "*G, /gɔɔ/ Gài; K, /kɔ̌ɔ/ Kài; K, /kɔ̌ɔ/ Kùuat.*"

2.3 Consonant Classes

Every consonant is categorised by being either Low, Middle or High class. Again, this is an arbitrary classification that is used alongside other factors, to help determine the tone of a syllable (section 5.3).

In this book, to assist you we colour-code all our consonants. Fortunately, it is a colour code that you will never forget as it is something that many of us see on a daily basis:

- **Red** is High [class]

- **Yellow** is Middle [class]

- **Green** is Low [class]

2.4   Final Consonant Sounds

The sounds shown in Table 2.2.1 are called *initial consonant* sounds. This is the sound the consonant makes when it's seen in the initial position in a word or a syllable. Naturally, if there are *initial consonant* sounds then it makes sense that there are also *final consonant* sounds: there are, eight of them: /ng/ (ง), /n/ (น), /m/ (ม), /i/ (ย), /o/ (ว), /k/ (ก), /t/ (ด), /p/ (บ).

With 44 consonants making just 21 initial consonant sounds and only 8 final consonant sounds it stands to reason that some consonants must have different *initial* and *final* sounds.

A Little Spice

For example, the word บุญ (bun, meaning *merit* or *virtue*) has Bɔɔ Bai-mái (บ) as the initial consonant (/b/), a vowel beneath the initial consonant (ุ) giving us the /u/ sound; and Yɔɔ Yǐng (ญ) as the final consonant; but, though Yɔɔ Yǐng has an initial consonant sound of /y/, its sound when a final consonant is /n/.

Of course, it is necessary to know the final consonant sound for a syllable in order to determine the correct tone, but we also need to know the type of sound each makes; and, to do this, *final consonant sounds* are further divided into *sonorant* and *stop* finals.

2.4.1   Sonorant and Stop Finals

Sonorant Finals

Sonorant finals are sounds that are fully voiced, e.g. the words, *song* or *drum*. When you say these you will feel your larynx vibrate (get a native Thai speaker to help you if you need to).

There are five sonorant finals in the Thai language.

Table 2.4.1 - Sonorant Finals

Consonant	Final Sound
ง	**/ng/**
ญ ณ น ร ล and ฬ	**/n/**
ม	**/m/**
ย	**/i/**
ว	**/o/**

As can be seen in the table above, the final consonant sound /n/ is made by a total of six different consonants. The following list shows examples of words containing the sonorant final consonants listed above:

- วาง (waang - *put down, place*)
- พาน (paan - *tray*)
- หาร (hǎan - *divide, share*)
- ผอม (pɔ̌ɔm - *thin, slim*)
- คอย (kɔɔi - *wait*)
- กาว (gaao - *glue, gum*).

Stop Finals

The three remaining final sounds are called stop final consonant sounds and are unaspirated. Think of saying the word *stop!* The /p/ is aspirated. However, if you unaspirate/shorten the 'p' so it sounds more like 'b', the word becomes similar to *stob;* here the letter itself is still **p** but there is no final stress on the final consonant.

You can test this by holding up a piece of paper in front on your mouth. Say the word *stop,* the paper should move. Next, say the word *stob* and, as the final consonant is unaspirated, the paper should be stationary.

The following table shows the stop final consonants and their corresponding sounds.

Table 2.4.2 - Stop Finals

Consonant	Final Sound
ก ข ค and ฆ	/k/
จ ฉ ช ซ ฌ ญ ฏ ฎ ฐ ฑ ฒ ด ต ถ ท ธ ศ ษ and ส	/t/
บ ป ผ ฝ พ ฟ and ภ	/p/

For example:

- มาก (mâak - *much, a lot*)
- นาค (nâak - *mythological serpent*)
- บาด (bàat - *cut*)
- ประเทศ (bprà-têet - *country, nation*)
- ชอบ (chɔ̂ɔp - *like*)
- ปรารภ (bpraa-róp - *introduction, remark* or *express concern*).

Note: even though all consonants have a final sound, not all consonants are used in the final position; but, unfortunately, you still need to learn them.

(Refer to Appendix A for the full list of initial and final consonant sounds).

3. Vowels

Vowel is pronounced sà-rà (ส-ระ) in Thai and is followed by the vowel name/sound itself, e.g. sà-rà am (-ํา) is written สระ -ํา and the vowel sound is written as /am/ (though it sounds similar to /um/ as in *umbrella*).

There are two types of basic vowel: short vowel and long vowel, the difference is in the length and this vowel length can be another factor for determining syllable tone (refer to section 5.3, Determining Tone).

Vowel sounds are written in the same way as consonant sounds but we need a method to differentiate between short and long. We do this with simple vowels by repeating the vowel sound when it is long, e.g. for sà-rà a (สระ -ะ), a short vowel, we write /a/; and for sà-rà aa (สระ -า), a long vowel, we write /aa/.

Note: The majority of the time, the sound is the same and it's just a longer vowel (approximately 2-3 times as long as a rough guide). But, as with any pronunciation, if you are unsure, it is advisable to seek assistance from a Thai friend.

3.1 Short and Long Vowels

Thai vowels can be placed in front of, above, after, and below a consonant. If no consonant is present, the hyphen (-) is used to represent where a consonant would be written [in relation to the vowel].

3.1.1   Simple Vowels

Table 3.1.2 lists all the common, long and short simple vowels

Table 3.1.2 - Short and Long Vowels

Short Vowel			Long Vowel		
Vowel	**Sound**	**Sounds Like**	**Vowel**	**Sound**	**Sounds Like**
The 4 vowels to the right can be short or long but are considered long for tone purposes.			-ำ	/am/	umbrella
			ไ-	/ai/	knight
			ใ-	/ai/	fly
			เ-า	/ao/	mouse
-ะ	/a/	puffin	-า	/aa/	palm
-ิ	/i/	lip	-ี	/ii/	steeple
-ึ	/ʉ/	push-up	-ื	/ʉʉ/	bloom
-ุ	/u/	crook	-ู	/uu/	boot
เ-ะ	/e/	net	เ-	/ee/	bed
แ-ะ	/ɛ/	trap	แ-	/ɛɛ/	bad
โ-ะ	/o/	cot	โ-	/oo/	ghost
เ-าะ	/ɔ/	slot	-อ	/ɔɔ/	awful

Some vowel sounds have no comparable sound in English and all given examples are sounds as close to the Thai sounds as the English language allows.

Particularly different (and difficult) are sà-rà /ʉ/ and /ʉʉ/. The sound for these has to come from your throat, similar to when you hiccup. The sound must be kept short (/ʉ/, but longer with /ʉʉ/) and it must come from the throat (not the mouth). Also, your mouth should be open slightly (just!).

We appreciate this sounds difficult, but we have the full complement of sounds in the Learn Thai Alphabet application, available from **www.learn-thaialphabet.com**.

You may have noticed that in Table 3.1.2 there are two vowels that make the /ai/ sound:

- Sà-rà **ai mái-má-lai** (ไ-), and
- Sà-rà **ai mái-múan** (ใ-).

Both produce exactly the same sound but there are only twenty occurrences of sà-rà ai mái-múan (ใ-) in the Thai language. A full list of these words is in Appendix C.2.

3.1.3   Complex Vowels

Table 3.1.4 lists the remaining 12 vowels. These vowels are formed by combining two or more short or long vowels.

The four shaded short vowels are <u>very</u> uncommon in Thai; and you will rarely encounter any words which use them.

Table 3.1.4 - Complex Vowels

Short Vowel			Long Vowel		
Vowel	**Sound**	**Sounds Like**	**Vowel**	**Sound**	**Sounds Like**
เ-อะ	/ə/	above	เ-อ	/əə/	early
เ-ียะ	/ia/	ria	เ-ีย	/iia/	reindeer
เ-ือะ	/ɯa/	newer	เ-ือ	/ɯɯa/	skua
-ัวะ	/ua/	buat	-ัว	/uua/	pure
ฤ	/rɯ/	rook	ฤๅ	/rɯɯ/	root
ฦ	/lɯ/	look	ฦๅ	/lɯɯ/	looney

3.2 Consonants and Vowels / Vowel Sounds

There are three consonants in the Thai alphabet that can function as consonants, vowels, or provide vowel sounds: Yɔɔ Yák (ย), Wɔɔ Wɛ̌ɛn (ว) and ɔɔ Àang (อ).

They form the following vowel sounds:

Table 3.2.1 Consonant Vowel Sounds

Consonant	Initial Consonant Sound	Final Consonant or Vowel Sound
Wɔɔ Wɛ̌ɛn (ว)	/w/	/o/ or /ua/
ɔɔ Àang (อ)	/ɔɔ/	/ɔɔ/
Yɔɔ Yák (ย)	/y/	/i/

Wɔɔ Wɛ̌ɛn (ว) and ɔɔ Àang (อ) can be used as vowels in their own right, i.e. on their own; however, when Wɔɔ Wɛ̌ɛn (ว) is found between two consonants, it adopts the short form of sà-rà ◌ัว and is pronounced /uua/, as shown in the first example below. Also, Yɔɔ Yák (ย) provides a vowel <u>sound</u> when it is preceeded by sà-rà เ-อ, (it forms เ-อย); and, as shown in the last 2 examples, the form is then reduced to เ-ย:

- บวม (buuam - *swollen*)
- ห่อ (hɔ̀ɔ - *parcel, package*)
- พ่อ (pɔ̂ɔ - *father*)
- เคย (kəəi - *use to*)
- เนย (nəəi - *butter*).

Note: The actual sound that เ-ย makes is difficult to express in English, but the closest vowel sound is /əə/ as in d**a**y.

*
In these few short pages you've been faced with 44 consonants, stop final consonants and sounds, sonorant finals, 32 vowels, monothongs, dipthongs, tripthongs, etc. Remember, as with all sections of this book, don't expect to learn it all at once, take your time, work on those parts you are comfortable with and use the other areas as guides or for background reading. Go at your own pace!

Learning the Thai Alphabet the Easy Way

If this all feels like a tall order, then rest assured that you're not alone. If you want to learn the alphabet a much faster way, then check out:

Learn Thai Alphabet with Memory Aids to Your Great Adventure and the **Learn Thai Alphabet application**.

Guaranteed to take your pain away!

"Well, I agree that your app and those posts are like a speed-of-light catalyst in terms teaching one the Thai script and reading it within literally two days (in my experience) which I find extraordinary..."

Emiliusz Smorczewski, Illinois, USA, 9th July 2013

www.learnthaialphabet.com

Erawan Shrine, Bangkok

Speaking Thai

4. Grammar

We don't cover a huge amount of grammar (wai-yaa-gɔɔn, ไว-ยา-กรณ์) in this book, just enough for you find your feet. Fortunately, the sentence structure in Thai is the same as that used in English:

Subject + Verb + Object

For example: *He likes rugby - kǎo chɔ̀ɔp rák-bîi* (เขา ชอบ รัก-บี้)

However, there are a number of differences in other grammar areas and we'll cover the main ones here.

Articles

Unlike English, which relies heavily on articles (*a, an* or *the*), Thai can be used with or without them and the grammar will still be correct, e.g. "*Where is the dog?*", is "*Where is dog*" or actually "*dog is where?*" (*sù-nák yùu tîi-nǎi* - สุ-นัข อยู่ ที่-ไหน).

*
  There are no **hyphens** in Thai script, none. Every one you see in this book has been added to aid you in identifying and reading Thai script.

4.1 Verbs and Tense

There are no verb, noun, or pronoun inflections in Thai and when you are talking about numbers, case, tense, or gender change, etc., additional words are used to indicate the exact meaning.

For example, verb tense itself does not change but the meaning is determined by the addition of extra word(s). Using the expression, *I drink beer...* pǒm dùum biia (ผม ดื่ม เบียร์) as an example:

1. Present Tense

   If you are in the process of doing something the word *gam-lang* (กำลัง) is used, e.g.

   I am drinking beer - pǒm gam-lang dùum biia (ผม กำ-ลัง ดื่ม เบียร์)

2. Past Tense

   If you have finished an action, i.e. it is complete, you use the word *already* - lέεo (แล้ว) at the end of the sentence, e.g.

   I drank beer - pǒm dùum biia lέεo (ผม ดื่ม เบียร์ แล้ว).

3. Future Tense

   If an action is going to happen in the future then we precede the verb with *will* - jà (จะ).

   *I will (or I shall) drink bee*r - pǒm jà dùum biia (ผม จะ ดื่ม เบียร์)

4.2 To Be

In English, we use the verb '*To be*' for a number of different situations such as "*I am 21 years old,*" or, "*I am over here!*" Thai has four methods of referring to '*to be*':

1. *yùu* (อยู่), is used when referring to a place or location.

2. *bpen* (เป็น), is used when referring to someone or something.

3. *kuu* (คือ), is also used when referring to someone or something.

4. *mii* (มี), is used similar to "*There is/there are*".

4.2.1 Location

Yùu (อยู่) is used when we are referring to a place or a location, for example:

- "I am over here," - *pŏm yùu tîi-nîi* (ผม อยู่ ที่-นี่)
- "Where are you?" - *kun yùu tîi-nǎi* (คุณ อยู่ ที่-ไหน).

4.2.2 Someone or Something

Bpen (เป็น) and *kʉʉ* (คือ) are used when talking about someone or something. They should only be used when linking a pronoun or a noun to another noun.

First of all, neither *bpen* or *kʉʉ* are utilised as linking verbs when used with an adjective. For example, using the sentence, "*I am hungry.*"

If you said "*pŏm bpen hĭo*" (ผม เป็น หิว) (pronoun + verb + adjective), this would be incorrect, the correct saying is "*pŏm hĭo*" (ผม หิว), "I hungry."

You wouldn't use *kʉʉ* (คือ) for the same reason.

Kʉʉ

Kʉʉ is used when referring to a noun or when you need to describe the meaning of the noun; it is also used similar to *e.g.* or *i.e.* in English. For example:

- "*Nîi kʉʉ à-rai?*" (นี่ คือ อะ-ไร) - "*What is this?*"
- "*Nîi kʉʉ bpàak-gaa,*" (นี่ คือ ปาก-กา) - "*This is a pen.*"
- "*Gâo-îi kʉʉ à-rai,*" (เก้า-อี้ คือ อะไร) - "*What is a chair?*"
- "*Gâo-îi kʉʉ tîi-nâng sǎm-ràp nâng kon sǎa-mâat klʉʉan-yáai dâi,*" (เก้า-อี้ คือ ที่-นั่ง สำ-หรับ 1 คน สา-มารถ เคลื่อน-ย้าย ได้) - "*A chair is a moveable seat for one person to sit on.*"

- *"Nîi kɯɯ bâan kɔ̌ɔng-chǎn,"* (นี่ คือ บ้าน ของ-ฉัน) - *"This is my home."*

- *"Nân kɯɯ rót kɔ̌ɔng-krai,"* (นั่น คือ รถ ของ-ใคร) - *"Whose car is that?"*

Bpen

Bpen is used when the subject and object are related. It is always used with occupation, nationality, disease, status/position or ownership, e.g.

- *"Kǎo bpen nák-bin,"* (เขา เป็น นัก-บิน) - *"He is a pilot."*

- *"Pǒm bpen nák-riian,"* (ผม เป็น นัก-เรียน) - *"I am a student."*

- *"Kǎo bpen kon jiin,"* (เขา เป็น คน จีน) - *"He is Chinese."*

- *"Chǎn bpen kâi,"* (ฉัน เป็น ไข้) - *"I have a fever."*

- *"Pǒm bpen kon sòot,"* (ผม เป็น คน โสด) - *"I am a single man."*

- *"Nân bpen rót kɔ̌ɔng-krai,"* (นั่น เป็น รถ ของ-ใคร) - *"Whose car is that?"*

You can see that the last example here is also used in the list under *kɯɯ*. There is a fine line between using *kɯɯ* and *bpen* and this comes with experience.

4.2.3   Mii

Mii (มี) is used in simple tense sentences where the meaning is *there is, there are*, etc. For example:

- *"Mii nák-riian yîi-sìp kon nai chán-riian."* (มี นัก-เรียน ยี่-สิบ คน ใน ชั้น-เรียน) - *"There are twenty students in class."*

- *"Kǎo mii nák-riian yîi-sìp kon nai chán-riian."* (เขา มี นัก-เรียน ยี่-สิบ คน ใน ชั้น-เรียน) - *"She has twenty students in class."*

4.3 Questions

In Thai language, the only difference between an affirmative and an interrogative sentence is the interrogative sentence uses an interrogative word either at the beginning or, more commonly, at the end of a sentence.

For example, the affirmative sentence, "*You work hard,*" (*kun tam-ngaan nàk* - คุณ ทำ-งาน หนัก) becomes the interrogative sentence by adding the question word, "*No*" at the end of the sentence.

This then becomes, "*Do you work hard?*" or actually, "*You work hard, no?*" (*kun tam-ngaan nàk măi* - คุณ ทำ-งาน หนัก ไหม).

4.4 Possession

The words *bpen kɔ̌ɔng* (เป็น ของ) - *belong* are used to indicate ownership or possession of an object or item.

For example, mine is *kɔ̌ɔng pǒm/chăn* (ของ ผม/ฉัน), yours is *kɔ̌ɔng kun* (ของ คุณ), his/hers is *kɔ̌ɔng kǎo* (ของ เขา), etc.

To say, "*The book is his,*" or, "*The book belongs to him,*" would be *năng-sǔu bpen kɔ̌ɔng kǎo* (หนัง-สือ เป็น ของ เขา).

4.5 Adjectives

Adjectives come after the noun that they are modifying, e.g. *The red car* becomes '*car red*' - *rót sǐi dɛɛng* (รถ สี แดง).

When Thai people speak to each other they will very often leave out words if the meaning of their sentence is unambiguous.

This can be confusing to a learner but is common in many languages, e.g. "Where is the bathroom?" (*hɔ̂ɔng nám yùu tîi-nǎi* - ห้อง น้ำ อยู่ ที่-ไหน), can be heard as just, "*Hɔ̂ɔng nám yùu nǎi.*"

Here we have the Thai words for bathroom, *hɔ̂ɔng nám: hɔ̂ɔng* (ห้อง) means room, and *nám* (น้ำ) means water.

Similarly, as the word for sleep is *nɔɔn* (นอน), the sleeping room - the bedroom - is *hɔ̂ɔng nɔɔn* (ห้อง นอน); and, as the Thai word for food is *aa-hǎan* (อา-หาร) the dining or eating room is *hɔ̂ɔng aa-hǎan* (ห้อง อา-หาร).

5. Tone

Thai is a tonal language and, as was mentioned before, every <u>syllable</u> has one of 5 tones: Low, Mid, High, Rising and Falling.

You may think that it would be logical for tone class to coincide with consonant class, e.g. high tone = high class consonants, low tone = low class but, unfortunately, it doesn't.

As mentioned briefly before, consonant class is an arbitrary classification that is used to group the consonants. It may well happen that a *syllable* with a Middle Class consonant is pronounced mid tone but this is due to other factors and not solely because of the consonant class.

Four factors affect the tone of a syllable:

1. If the syllable has a tone mark above the initial consonant (section 5.1)

2. The class of the consonant (section 5.2);

3. The vowel length (table 3.1.2)

4. Whether the end/final sound is a *live syllable* or a *dead syllable* (section 5.2).

First of all, we'll look at tone marks.

5.1 Tone Marks

There are four tone marks in Thai script. With the exception of consonant clusters (covered in Appendix C.4) tone marks are always written above the initial consonant of a syllable [or a superscript vowel, if present].

The following table shows the tone marks used in Thai script:

Table 5.1.1 -Tone Marks

Tone Mark	Name		When written above the consonant class (shown below), that syllable will produce the tone shown:		
			Low Class	Middle Class	High Class
่	Mái èek	ไม้ เอก	Falling Tone (^)	Low (\)	Low (\)
้	Mái too	ไม้ โท	High Tone (/)	Falling (^)	Falling (^)
๊	Mái dtrii	ไม้ ตรี	High (/)		
๋	Mái jàt-dtà-waa	ไม้ จัต-วา	Rising Tone (v)		

Note: when a tone mark is present, *it overrules all other tone rules*.

For example: the word ป่า (pronounced bpàa, low tone) means '*forest, jungle*' and is comprised of *Bpɔɔ Bplaa* (ป), *mái èek* (-่) and *sà-rà* aa (-า).

Bpɔɔ Bplaa (ป) is a Middle Class consonant and, from the table above, we see a Middle Class consonant + mái èek = **low tone**.

Once you have learnt the tone mark rules, it is fairly easy to see what the tone of a particular syllable will be.

The main problem is that if no tone mark is present then the tone has to be calculated. This is incredibly slow at first and can be a major hurdle.

In English, when we learn a word we have to remember the pronunciation, the spelling, and the meaning; Thai is exactly the same but you must also place additional emphasis on learning the correct tone.

Aids to Memory I - Tone Marks

Many find it difficult to remember the tone/tone mark rules so we've included the following images and 'stories' to assist you; these are the memory aids that Russ created and uses — we hope they help.

Bear in mind that all memory aids are there to help you learn and recall information. If these don't make sense to you then just try and come up with your own.

- **Mái èek** (-) - this looks like a bomb dropped from a warplane.

  When the plane flies on *high* or *middle* altitude bombing missions (*high* or *middle* class consonants) the bomb explodes at *low level* (read *low tone*).

  When the plane is on a *low* altitude bombing mission (read *low* class consonant) it uses pinpoint accuracy and can drop the bomb into holes and the bomb *falls* deeper into the ground (read *falling* tone).

  Therefore:

  Middle & High [class consonants] = **Low** [tone]; **Low** [class consonant] = **Falling** [tone].

- **Mái too** (-) - imagine this as the head of a sickle (or a scythe) used in a peasant rebellion.

  The low class peasants revolt and the *middle* and *high* classes *fall* from grace; the *low classes* now elevate themselves to become *high* class.

Therefore: **Middle** & **High** = **Fall**ing, **Low** = [the new] **High.**

- **Mái dtrii** (-́) - imagine this shape as a crown on the head of royalty - the *high*est level in social status (**high** tone).

- **Mái jàt-dtà-waa** (-̆)- this is like a *rising* star, twinkling in the night sky (**rise** [ing] tone).

5.2 Live and Dead Syllables

We have spoken about sonorant final consonants, stop final consonants, short vowels and long vowels, now we need to understand what type of syllable endings there are, as these are necessary for calculating tone; there are two types: dead syllable, and live syllable:

- A **dead syllable** is a syllable that ends with a **short vowel** or ends with a **stop final** consonant.

- A **live syllable** is a syllable that ends with a **long vowel** or a **sonorant final** consonant.

For example:

- จะ (jà – *will*). Sà-rà **a** (-ะ /a/) is a short vowel (Table 3.1.2), therefore this is a dead syllable.

- จัด (jàt – *arrange, prepare*). Dɔɔ Dèk (ด) is a stop final consonant (Table 2.4.2) and therefore this is a dead syllable.

- ไป (bpai – *go, leave*). Sà-rà ai (ไ- /ai/) is a long vowel (Table 3.1.2) and this is a live syllable.

- ยาว (yaao – *long*). Wɔɔ Wɛ̌ɛn (ว) is a sonorant final consonant (Table 2.4.1) and this is a live syllable.

5.3 Determining Tone

To reiterate, from section 5.1, where ***tone marks are not present*** we calculate tone from:

1. The class of the consonant (section 5.2 and Table 2.2.1)

2. Whether the vowel is short or long (section 3.1.2).

3. Whether the final consonant is a sonorant or stop final (section 2.4.1).

In addition, for <u>Low Class</u> consonants only, if the syllable is dead, the tone will depend on whether the vowel is short or long.

Table 5.3.1 - Calculating Tone

Syllable Type	Consonant Class		
	High Class	Middle Class	Low Class
Dead Syllables	Low Tone (\)	Low Tone (\)	Short Vowel: High Tone (/)
			Long Vowel: Falling Tone (^)
Live Syllables	Rising Tone (v)	Middle Tone	Middle Tone

For example:

- รับ (ráp – *receive*). **Low Class** consonant (Rɔɔ Ruua - ร) + short vowel (-ั) + stop final consonant/dead syllable (Bɔɔ Bai-mái - บ) = High tone.

- มาก (mâak – *much, many*). **Low Class** consonant (Mɔɔ Máa - ม) + long vowel (-า) + stop final consonant/dead syllable (Gɔɔ Gài - ก) = Falling tone.

- ฟาง (faang – *straw*). **Low Class** consonant (Fɔɔ Fan - ฟ) + long vowel (-า) + sonorant consonant/live syllable (Ngɔɔ Nguu - ง) = Middle tone.

- ปิด (bpìt – *close, hide, shut, turn off*). **Middle Class** consonant (Bpɔɔ Bplaa - ป) + short vowel (-ิ) + stop final consonant/dead syllable (Dɔɔ Dèk - ด) = Low tone.

- ขวา (kwǎa – *right*). **High Class** consonant (Kɔɔ Kài - ข) + long vowel/live syllable (-า) = Rising tone.

At first (and understandably) the thought of remembering these tone rules may be a little daunting, but all is not lost as there are some other memory aids that Russ also created to help you.

Aids To Memory II - Tone Rules

Here are the acronyms that Russ uses to remember the tone rules:

- **H**arry **D**rinks **L**ager (**H**igh [class consonant] + **D**ead [syllable] = **L**ow [tone]) **HDL**
- **H**arry **L**ikes **R**ed Stripe (**H**igh + **L**ive = **R**ising) **HLR**
- **M**ike **D**rinks **L**ager (**M**iddle + **D**ead = **L**ow) **MDL**
- **M**ike **L**ikes **M**iller (**M**iddle + **L**ive = **M**iddle) **MLM**
- **L**esley **D**rinks **SH**andy (**L**ow + **D**ead + **Sh**ort [vowel] = **H**igh) **LDSH**
- **L**esley **D**rinks **L**ager **F**ast (**L**ow + **D**ead + **L**ong [vowel] = **F**alling) **LDLF**
- **L**esley **L**ikes **M**iller (**L**ow + **L**ive = **M**iddle) **LLM**

Thus, using the examples from section 5.3:

- รับ (ráp) – Low Class consonant + Dead syllable and Short vowel = High

- มาก (mâak) – Low Class consonant + Dead syllable and Long vowel = Falling

- ฟาง (faang) – Low Class consonant + Live syllable = Middle tone

- ปิด (bpìt) – Middle Class consonant + Dead syllable = Low

- ขวา (kwǎa) – High Class consonant + Live syllable = Rising.

Try and come up with your own.[2]

Note: These and all the memory aids for learning the consonants, verbs and tone rules can be found in volume 2 of *Quest: 'Learn Thai Alphabet with Memory Aids to Your Great Adventure'* or **The Learn Thai Alphabet Application** at **http://www.learnthaialphabet.com**.

---

2. The authors support the responsible consumption of alcohol and, please remember, this is an aid to memory whereas alcohol isn't.

Reading Thai

When most westerners look at Thai script for the first time they look for some kinds of clues or for any link or resemblance between Thai character shapes and their 'own' alphabets.

The shapes are unfamiliar and there are additional strange characters written above the consonants. There are other 'weird' shapes written above those and few spaces between the words: all told, there are very few clues and no familiar references. Don't worry though, all is not lost and the following sections contain some of the basic rules to help you.

6.   Rules for Reading Thai

One of the most confusing and off-putting features of Thai script is there are no spaces between words. Obviously, if you don't know where the words start and end, how can you possibly read them? As you can no doubt appreciate, the ability to identify syllables and words is fundamental to learning Thai.

In total, there are 8 rules for reading Thai and you need to learn them all as you will be using them constantly. Of course, as you progress, the process will become automatic but it does take a bit of time at first.

1. Every syllable starts with a consonant.

    Though the first character written in a syllable is not necessarily a consonant the consonant is <u>always</u> pronounced first.

2. A written vowel is always associated with a consonant.

    There are no 'free-standing' vowels, such as the vowels 'I' and 'A' in the English language. A vowel is always written 'around' a consonant.

3. A vowel is always written in the same place in relation to a consonant, it's position doesn't change.

   Some vowels are written before the consonant, some below, some above, and some after: but they are always written in the same position (section 7.1).

4. Sà-rà ใ-, ไ-, -ะ and -า are never followed by a final consonant.

5. Sà-rà am (-ำ) always marks the end of a syllable.

6. The following vowel is always followed by a final consonant: -ั

That's the first 6 of the 8 rules; but, as the remaining 2 are about unwritten vowels, we'll cover them in the appropriate sections (7.2.1 and 7.2.2).

7. Vowels

When a vowel is written it must have a consonant associated with it. Irrespective of where the vowel is written, the consonant/consonant sound is always spoken first (rules 1 & 3 from the six you have just learnt): remember Gài (ไก่, from Gɔɔ Gài - section 2)?

The vowel sound is always the same irrespective of the consonant it is used with, e.g. sà-rà -า /aa/ is always pronounced /aa/: gaa (กา - *crow*), raa (รา - *fungus*), maa (มา - *come*), etc.

First of all, we'll look at where vowels are written, this will help you in deciphering Thai script. In the following examples, once again, the hyphen (-) indicates the position where the consonant would be.

7.1 Where to Write Vowels

Vowels can be written before, above, below and after consonants.

Vowels Before

The following vowels always start a syllable:

เ -, แ -, โ -, ไ -, ใ-

e.g. เก่ง (gèeng - *skilled, talented*), แต่ (dtὲɛ - *but, since*), โมง (moong - *hour (daytime), o'clock*), ไม่ (mâi - *no*), ใจ (jai - *heart, mind, spirit*).

Vowels Above

These vowels are always written above an *initial* consonant:

-ิ, -ี, -ื, -ึ, -ั

e.g. อิ่ม (ìm - *full up*), อีก (ìik - *again, more*), อึ้ง (ûng - *quiet, tongue-tied*), อืด (ùut - *slow, tardy*),ทั้ง (táng - *all, entire, whole*).

Vowels Below

These vowels are always written below an *initial* consonant:

-ุ, -ู

e.g. ดุ (dù - *fierce, ferocious*), รู้ (rúu - *know (something)*).

Vowels After

The following vowels are always written after a consonant:

- ะ, -า, -ำ

e.g. จะ (jà - *will*), หา (hǎa - *search*), จำ (jam - *remember, recall, recognise*).

Complex vowels are those that are comprised of more than one vowel. However, each component vowel part is still written in the same place. You just need to work out what the vowel/vowel sound is.

For example, the word *riian* (เรียน - *study*) uses the dipthong vowel เ-ีย (sà-rà เ-ีย /**iia**/). Sà-rà เ-, sà-rà -ี and ย (Yɔɔ Yák) are written in their 'usual' place, you just need to remember the vowel sound.

If we replaced the ร in เรียน with ล (to give us เลียน, *liian - imitate, copy*) the vowel sound is exactly the same.

If you asked a Thai person to spell เรียน, you probably wouldn't hear "*Sà-rà /ee/, rɔɔ rʉʉa, sà-rà /ii/, yɔɔ yák, nɔɔ nǔu*", they would say "*Rɔɔ rʉʉa, sà-rà /iia/, nɔɔ nǔu.*" Clear, concise and little chance of error.

7.2 Unwritten Vowels

There are two unwritten vowels in Thai: sà-rà โ-ะ (/**o**/), as in '*tot* ' and sà-rà -ะ (/**a**/), as in '*up*'

7.2.1 Same Syllable

Unwritten โ-ะ (/**o**/) occurs between two consonants in the **same** syllable:

For example, in the personal pronoun ผม (pǒm - meaning *I, me,* used only by men) and in ฝน (fǒn - meaning *rain*).

Note: when the final consonant is Rɔɔ Rʉʉa (ร) then the unwritten vowel between two same syllable consonants is changed from sà-rà โ-ะ (/**o**/) to sà-rà -อ (/**ɔɔ**/).

For example:

- พร (*blessing*) is not pronounced /p/+/o/+/n/ it is pronounced /p/+/ɔɔ/+/n/ - /**pɔɔn**/.

- ศร (*arrow*) is pronounced /s/+/ɔɔ/ +/n/ - /**sɔɔn**/.

7.2.2   Different Syllable

Unwritten sà-rà -ะ (/a/) occurs between two **different** syllable consonants, e.g. สวัสดี (ส-วัส-ดี sà-wàt-dii - meaning *hello, good morning, good evening*, etc).

Note: With this different syllable rule, when the initial consonant of a syllable is Bɔɔ Bai-mái (บ) the unwritten vowel is pronounced /ɔɔ/ not /a/, e.g. wan pá-rɯ́-hàt-sà-bɔɔ-dii (วัน พ-ฤ-หั-ส-บ-ดี) - *Thursday.*

7.3   Mái Hăn-aa-gàat

In the example above, we see the character ◌ั. This is called *mái hăn-aa-gàat* (ไม้ หัน-อา-กาศ) and it gives us a [short] /a/ sound, which is exactly the same sound as unwritten vowel sà-rà -ะ (/a/).

Sà-rà /ua/ (◌ัว)

Referring to Table 3.1.4, you will see that sà-rà ◌ัว (/uua/) is comprised of *mái hăn-aa-gàat* and wɔɔ wɛ̆ɛn (◌ัว).

When sà-rà ◌ัว (/uua/) has a final consonant, *mái hăn-aa-gàat* becomes an unwritten vowel; sà-rà ◌ัว /uua/ is still pronounced the same, e.g.

- รวย (ruai - *rich*)
- สวน (sŭan - *garden*)
- บวช (buat - *ordain, become a monk*).

8.   Silent Consonants

When you listen to the Thai language you will hear vowel sounds being spoken without an apparent consonant sound. Now this may appear to contravene rules 1 & 2 (in section 6) but it doesn't: there are 'silent' consonants in the Thai alphabet.

Although all syllables must start with a consonant (as per rule 1), some consonants can be silent (we write a silent consonant as /-/). As there is now a consonant present, a vowel can be placed (rule 2).

There are two consonants that can be silent: ออ Àang (อ อ่าง) and Hŏɔ Hìip (ห หีบ). We will consider Hŏɔ Hìip first.

8.1   Hŏɔ Hìip

Hŏɔ Hìip (ห หีบ) is a **High Class** consonant that has two purposes. First of all, it produces the **/h/** sound when spoken; secondly it is used to modify the class of consonants. In this latter capacity it becomes a 'silent' consonant (/-/).

Looking in detail at sections 5.1, Tone Marks and 5.3, Calculating Tone you will see it is not possible to have a low tone with a **Low Class** consonant.

The following table shows some **Low Class** consonants with their corresponding **High Class** [sounding] equivalents:

Low Class Consonant & Sound	Corresponding High Class Consonant & Sound
(ค) Kɔɔ Kwaai **/k/**	(ข) Kŏɔ Kài **/k/**
(ช) Chɔɔ Cháang **/ch/**	(ฉ) Chŏɔ Chìng **/ch/**

The following Low Class consonants do not have a High Class equivalent: ง, ญ, น, ม, ย, ร, ล, ว.

But, by using Hɔ̌ɔ Hìip, the **Low Class** *initial consonant* is replaced with a 'silent' **High Class** initial consonant and becomes a **High Class** syllable.

Example 1

ลาย (laai - *design, pattern*): **L**ow Class [consonant] + **L**ive [syllable] = **M**id tone (**LLM**).

Whereas, by placing Hɔ̌ɔ Hìip in front of it, it now becomes:

หลาย (lǎai - *many, several*): **H**igh Class [consonant] + **L**ive [syllable] = **R**ising tone (**HLR**).

Example 2

มาด (mâat – *appearance or manner*): **L**ow Class + **D**ead syllable and **L**ong vowel = **F**alling tone (**LDLF**).

Golden Triangle, N Thailand

Using Hɔ̌ɔ Hìip, it now becomes:

หมาด (màat - *almost dry*): **H**igh Class + **D**ead syllable = **L**ow tone (**HDL**).

8.2 ออ Àang

ออ Àang (อ อ่าง) has a dual purpose: firstly it produces the /ɔɔ/ sound when spoken; and, secondly, it is used as a silent consonant/vowel (/-/).

We say consonant/vowel because although ออ Àang is the 43rd consonant it actually acts more like a vowel than a consonant. The 'silent' character-istic enables it to be used as a *vowel placement consonant*.

We will show two examples of ออ Àang:

1. acting as a voiced consonant/vowel

2. as a silent [vowel placement] consonant.

8.2.1   ออ Àang as a Voiced Consonant/Vowel

- กอด (gòot). This word means *embrace* or *hug*, and is comprised of: Goo Gài (ก), ออ Àang (อ) and Doo Dèk (ด).

    Goo Gài as an initial consonant gives the /g/ sound; ออ Àang is voiced as /ɔɔ/; and Doo Dèk as a [stop] final consonant gives a /t/ sound.

    Tone rules state Middle Class consonant (ก) + Dead syllable (ด) = Low Tone (section 5.3 and section 2.4.1) (MDL).

This word is pronounced /gòot/, low tone.

Note: For this example, we have to ask ourselves what actually is ออ Àang doing here, is it a consonant or a vowel?

If you remember, ออ Àang produces the /ɔɔ/ sound whether it is acting as a consonant or as a vowel (Table 2.2.1 or Table 3.1.2).

In addition, unlike English, every Thai word needs at least one consonant and one vowel. Thus, if the อ in กอด is acting as a consonant then the word is comprised of three written consonants **and**, if you remember the unwritten vowel rules from section 7.2, it would also have to have two of these.

This would then give us an unwritten /a/ between ก & อ and an unwritten /o/ between อ & ด. If we write this out phonetically it would be more like /g/ + /a/ + /ɔɔ/ + /o/ + /t/ (ga-ɔɔ-ot), and is wrong. Therefore, in this example, อ has to be acting as a vowel.

8.2.2   ออ Àang as a Silent [Vowel Placement] Consonant

- อีก (ìik). The word means *again*.

  The /ii/ part of the word comes from [silent] ออ Àang (/-/) and the vowel sà-rà ◌ี (/ii/). The /k/ comes from Gɔɔ Gài (ก) acting as a final consonant.

  The tone for this word is Middle Class consonant (อ) + Dead syllable (ก) = Low tone (MDL)

- อาหาร (อา-หาร - aa-hǎan). This means *"food"*.

  This word has two syllables. In the first syllable (อา), ออ Àang is silent and enables the placement of sà-rà -า (/aa/).

  When the silent consonant is used, the only sound is the vowel sound /aa/.

  This syllable's tone is calculated as:

  Middle Class consonant (อ) + Live syllable (-า) = Mid tone (MLM)

  The second syllable is หาร (/hǎan/).

  The pronunciation of this syllable is straightforward and is pronounced rising tone:

  High Class consonant (ห) + Live Syllable (remember Rɔɔ Rʉʉa as a final consonant gives the /n/ sonorant sound) = Rising tone (HLR).

- อาหารเช้า (อา-หาร เช้า - aa-hǎan cháo). This three syllable word means *"breakfast"* and is derived from the Thai word for *food* and the word for *morning* (เช้า - cháo).

  The last syllable is high tone from Low Class consonant (ช) + Mái Too (◌้).

  Note: the word for *noon/midday* is *t̂iang* (เที่ยง), therefore *lunch* is *aa-hǎan t̂iang*.

The Thai word for *dinner* is *aa-hăan yen* (อาหาร เย็น) and this just needs a short explanation.

The word for evening is *dtɔɔn yen* (ตอน เย็น): *dtɔɔn* is a word commonly used to denote a time period, and *yen* means late afternoon, evening or dusk. *Dtɔɔn* is dropped when there is no ambiguity.

"Have you eaten yet?"

Rice is a huge part of Thai food culture and is eaten with most meals. You may hear some Thai people say, "*Gin kâao lέεo rŭu yang?*" (กิน ข้าว แล้ว หรือ ยัง) when they meet a friend around a meal-time - as opposed to *sà-wàt-dii* (สวัสดี); this translates as "*Eat rice already yet?*" or "*Have you eaten yet?*" and was the traditional greeting before *sà-wàt-dii* was introduced. It is still used by some, mainly older, people today.

Breakfast can also be referred to as *kâao cháo* (ข้าว เช้า); lunch as *kâao tîiang* (ข้าว เที่ยง); and, dinner as *kâao yen* (ข้าว เย็น).

ɔɔ Àang Changing Consonant Class

Additionally, ɔɔ Àang is seen as the first consonant in certain words such as:

- yàak (อยาก) - *would like*
- yàang (อย่าง) - *as, like*.

In both examples ɔɔ Àang is acting as a silent consonant, similar to Hɔɔ Hìip, but each word now becomes Middle Class: without ɔɔ Àang, each word would be Low Class (from the initial consonant Yɔɔ Yák).

Without ɔɔ Àang we would have yâak (ยาก) - *hard, difficult* and yâang (ย่าง) - *grill*. Note the tones: falling tone for the former (remember LDLF), and falling tone for the latter (mái èek + low class consonant).

9. Shortening Vowels

Thai has two methods of shortening a word and its pronunciation: firstly, with ◌ (mái-dtài-kúu), and secondly with sà-rà - ะ (/a/).

9.1 Mái-dtài-kúu (◌)

The character ◌ is called mái-dtài-kúu (ไม้-ไต่-คู้).

Mái-dtài-kúu is used with the vowels sà-rà เ- (/ee/) and sà-rà แ- (/ɛɛ/) to shorten the word.

Shortening sà-rà เ-

Using the word เบน (been - *turn away, change direction*), and adding mái-dtài-kúu gives us เบ็น (Ben - *man's name*).

With one exception, mái-dtài-kúu must have a final consonant associated with it as the syllable cannot end with just ◌; this exception is with the word ก็ (Gô – *also*). ก็ is pronounced with the inherent (อ) vowel sound.

As an aid to assist you in pronunciation, the length of the vowel when mái-dtài-kúu is used is similar to the length of saying the word '*n*' in English.

Shortening sà-rà แ-

แล็ปท็อป - this is how *laptop* is spelt in Thai (แล็ป-ท็อป - *lép-tɔ́p*).

9.2 Sà-rà -ะ

The second method is by using -ะ (sà-rà /a/).

Sà-rà -ะ can be used to shorten the long vowel sà-rà แ- and other complex vowels (refer to Table 3.1.4), e.g. และ (lέ - *and*): without the 'shortener' this word would be แล (lɛɛ - *look, see, glance*).

Sà-rà -ะ is <u>always</u> at the end of a syllable, it's a **terminal vowel**.

10. Last Consonant/First Consonant

As we have seen, there are a few consonants that have one sound as an initial consonant and a different sound as a final consonant. There are also a number of words in the language where words have been joined together and the final consonant of one syllable also acts as the initial consonant of the next. This way the consonant is written only once yet fulfils both the initial and final consonant position.

One example of this is in the word ผลไม้ (pǒn-lá-mái - *fruit*).

It is spelt as if it should be pǒn-mái (ผลไม้) but Lɔɔ Ling (ล) provides the final consonant sound /n/ at the end of the first syllable and then provides its initial consonant sound of /l/ for the middle syllable. The unwritten vowel /a/ (section 7.2) gives us the vowel for the middle syllable (ผน-ละ-ไม้ - this is how phonetic Thai is written - pǒn-lá-mái).

Another example is the word พจนานุกรม (pót-jà-naa-nú-grom - *dictionary*). Here, Jɔɔ Jaan provides the final consonant sound /t/ at the end of the first syllable and then its initial consonant sound /j/ for the second syllable (in phonetic Thai it is written as พด-จะ-นา-นุ-กรม).

You need to be aware that there are a number of words in Thai which do not conform to the rules shown. Without knowing the actual word itself, it is unlikely that you would be able to work out the correct pronunciation. In these cases you need to know the word and its meaning.

Writing Thai

If you have never written Thai script before then initially it will seem very difficult and cumbersome: this is, of course, purely due to a lack of familiarity and practice. Russ's own experience was that he struggled with most of the characters, was very slow, his handwriting looked untidy and scratchy and his end result was very unimpressive.

Though he persevered for a time, he couldn't master the 'beak' of Gɔɔ Gài; the 'loops' on Kɔɔ Rá-kang and Chɔɔ Chəə just tied him in knots; and, as for dɔɔ and dtɔɔ... well forget it, it confused him!

On one particular break, he went outside and walked down the soi, and as the wafts of Pàd Tai, Gɛɛng Kĭiao Wăan Gài, Sôm-dtam or Gŭai dtĭiao hit him from the multitude of street vendors, he glanced about and saw the many hand-written signs. It was then that he realised that very few of us actually can or do write in the style of the Times New Roman or Bookman Old Style fonts [Thai-equivalent of course].

It was then he asked Duangta for some writing assistance and she showed him how to write the Thai characters; and, it all came together.

Jomtien beach

11. How To Write Thai Characters

It is recommended that you start practising writing the Thai alphabet as soon as possible.

> It's an aside but, as part of Russ's studies at Ramkamhaeng University, you had to be able to write out the Thai alphabet. We appreciate that this may not necessarily be anything you're going to be doing, but if you're going to learn the language, then perhaps it's another good reason for starting early.

11.1 Consonant Practice

On the right hand page of each page spread, you will see a character drawn in the box:

Take a piece of tracing paper, cover the letter and then start drawing the shape of the character in the order of the indicating arrows. Keep going until you get the feel for the drawn shape. Where consonants have loops, always try and start with the loop and, where possible, complete the consonant in one stroke.

Note: When you draw a consonant, be aware of where the loop actually is. (left, right, above or below the actual line you are drawing). Its position is important as it is, in a number of cases, the only difference between writing Kɔɔ Kwaai (ค) and Dɔɔ Dèk (ด), or Kɔɔ Kon (ค) and Dtɔɔ Dtào (ต).

*
Try and master writing the consonants as they are written at the top of each page, it does take longer to learn but looks far neater.

11.2 Vowels

Refer to Appendix D for instructions on how to write the vowels correctly.

Page Layout

Now we will look at the layout of the story section. First of all the consonant main page.

12. Main Page

Each page spread of the book is one consonant of the Thai alphabet (as shown below).

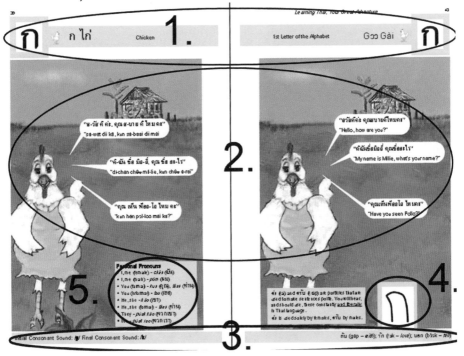

As you can see, it is broken down into five areas:

1. Header

2. Main dialogue

3. Footer

4. Writing Thai characters

5. Information Boxes.

The page is designed to ensure that all the information that you need is in front of you. It keeps you on the same page so that your concentration doesn't waver and your time is actually spent learning and not trying to find information.

12.1 Header

Your initial view shows you that the Header Bar is yellow. The colour of the bar is a memory aid to learning the consonant class. The yellow bar indicates this is a Middle Class consonant (section 5.2).

From the left you see:

1. The consonant character

2. A picture of the item, telling you what this item actually is, e.g. for Gɔɔ Gài, you see a picture of a chicken.

3. The name of the consonant (in Thai script): this is how you refer to it and how the word is pronounced.

4. The English meaning of the consonant letter.

Then, on the right hand page, still continuing on from the left:

5. Its position in the Thai alphabet (1 – 44, in English)

6. The transliterated name of the consonant

7. The picture

8. The consonant character.

12.2 Main Dialogue

Here we have the main dialogue of the book and there are two identical images facing you. First of all, we'll look at the left page.

12.2.1 Left Page

On the left page you have the information and dialogue given to you in transliterated Thai and in hyphenated, word-spaced Thai script. This introduces a number of common phrases and frequently used words to you and enables easy viewing of each syllable and word in Thai and quick following of the dialogue.

The transliterated Thai helps you to understand how to say the word by showing you its breakdown by syllable and its pronunciation.

The Thai script has been hyphenated to help you view and learn the individual syllables and words. We have also inserted commas into the Thai script to match the comma break in the transliterated text. This helps you to match the transliterated pronunciation to the actual Thai word.

All of these are only to assist you at this early stage, *there are no hyphenations or punctuation* in actual Thai script.

Hyphenated words will never be 100% accurate because many Thai words have unwritten vowels (section 7.2). Placing a hyphen immediately after a consonant may lead you to believe that the consonant is providing its own inherent sound <u>and</u> the vowel sound, it isn't; but, it's the only way we can indicate it.

For example, with the word สวัสดี (sàwàtdii - *hello*). We break this down by syllable to 'sà-wàt-dii'.

We hyphenate the first syllable between ส and ว, to give ส-ว[ส-ดี]. However, the first syllable is pronounced /**sà**/ as there is an unwritten '*a*' between the two consonants that are in different syllables.

You cannot tag the unwritten '*a*' in front of ว (as this would change the sound and the meaning of the word) so it has to read as if it belongs to the preceding consonant, ส. However, writing it in this manner incorrectly gives the impression that Sɔ̌ɔ Sʉ̌ʉa <u>alone</u> is giving us the /**sà**/ sound, whereas in fact it comes from a combination of ส **and** ว, the unwritten vowel rule. Alas, there is no other effective method of hyphenation and you need to be aware of this when reading any hyphenated and transliterated Thai.

12.2.2 Right Page

The drawing on the right page is identical to that on the left but this time the dialogue is in Thai script, *exactly as it would be written*, with the English translation beneath it.

This layout enables you to concentrate on the left page at first, learning the Thai script, the word shapes and the pronunciation. Then, with just a quick glance you can see how it would actually be written and obtain the meaning of the words, phrase or sentence without leaving your double-page spread.

Once you become more proficient you can just ignore the left page and read the Thai script on the right.

12.3 Footer Bar

Shown in the Footer Bar on the left-page is the sound that the consonant makes. Some consonants have only one sound irrespective of whether they are an initial or final consonant, others have different sounds, one as an initial consonant and the other when they are in the final consonant position. These will be shown here.

On the right-hand page are common words that use this particular consonant. They are written in Thai script, transliterated Thai and English to help you to expand your vocabulary, to familiarise yourself with Thai script, and to practice.

12.4 Information Boxes

As you progress through the book you will see information boxes on some of the pages.

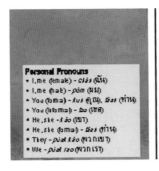

These boxes are there to provide additional information to assist you in learning the language, expanding your vocabulary and by providing various cultural and other useful information.

Let's continue with the consonant story; but, first, a quick note about it.

About the Consonant Story

When you go through the consonant story pages, you will realise fairly quickly that there is no start, middle, or end to this story. If you've looked on the Internet for some other alternatives to help link the consonant order, then you've probably encountered the 'Thai Alphabet poem'.

This poem was created many years ago and all Thai children are taught it at an early age. Admittedly, it works great for them as a learning tool, but it isn't easy non-Thai learners: it certainly wasn't for Russ and, of all the non-Thai's we know, not one of them knows this poem.

As such, we wracked our brains to try and create some form of creditable alternative and, as the story we have created does help with this, as well as providing a very visual method of helping you to learn the consonants, their classes, their sounds, and their shapes, we believe it is of some use.

However, given the diversity and range of consonant meanings, and bearing in mind this is a beginners level, introductory book, it is impossible to have a meaningful story: for example, the first 4 consonants in order are chicken, then egg (at least it answers THAT question), then bottle, and water buffalo. So, though it may perhaps be no tall-order for a fable from Aesop, when the consonants later transition to: woman-decorative head-dress-spear-pedestal-giant's wife-old man-novice monk, etc., perhaps it may prove difficult after all.

Furthermore, when you then try and factor in the creation and introduction of simple to use, everyday Thai phrases on a single page, within the given space, while still endeavouring to make the material visually appealing and fun to learn...well, we hope you can both appreciate and understand the challenge faced. Of course, if it doesn't work for you, then we can only recommend the Thai alphabet poem as there isn't anything else.

Consonant Story

ก

 ก ไก่   Chicken

"ส-วัส-ดี ค่ะ, คุณ ส-บาย ดี ไหม คะ"

"sà-wàt-dii kâ, kun sà-baai dii măi ká."

"ดิ-ฉัน ชื่อ มิล-ลี่, คุณ ชื่อ อะ-ไร"

"dì-chăn chûu míl-lii, kun chûu à-rai"

"คุณ เห็น พอล-โล่ ไหม คะ"

"kun hĕn pɔɔl-lôo măi ká?"

Personal Pronouns
- I, me (female) - *dì-chăn* (ดิ-ฉัน)
- I, me (male) - *pŏm* (ผม)
- You (formal) - *kun* (คุณ), *tâan* (ท่าน)
- You (informal) - *təə* (เธอ)
- He, she - *kăo* (เขา)
- He, she (formal) - *tâan* (ท่าน)
- They - *púuak kăo* (พวกเขา)
- We - *púuak rao* (พวกเรา)

Initial Consonant Sound: /g/ Final Consonant Sound: /k/

1st Letter of the Alphabet   Gɔɔ Gài   ก

"สวัสดีค่ะ คุณสบายดีไหมคะ"
"Hello, how are you?"

"ดิฉันชื่อมิลลี่ คุณชื่ออะไร"
"My name is Millie, what's your name?"

"คุณเห็นพอลโล่ ไหมคะ"
"Have you seen Pollo?"

ค่ะ (kâ) and ครับ (kráp) are particles that are used to make sentences polite. You will hear and should use them constantly <u>and liberally</u> in Thai language. ค่ะ is used solely by females, ครับ by males.

กับ (gàp – *with*); รัก (rák – *love*); บอก (bɔ̀ɔk – *tell*)

ข ไข่

Egg

Thai uses **Subject** + **Verb** + **Object** for composing sentences.

Determiners, however, are rarely used, e.g. in English, we say, "A bottle and a letter!".

However in Thai it's, "kùat lɛ́ jòt-mǎai" (ขวด และ จด-หมาย) - literally, "*Bottle and letter*".

2nd Letter of the Alphabet

Kɔ̌ɔ Kài

ข

โข (kǒo – *very*); เขา (kǎo – *he*, *she*); แข่ง (kɛ̀ɛng – *race*); เลข (lêek - *number, digit*)

ฃ ขวด   Bottle

ผมชื่อทอมมี่
My name is Tommy

ผมเป็นคนอังกฤษ
I am English.

ผมอายุ 20 ปี
I am 20 years old

ผมอยู่ที่ลอนดอน
I live in London.

ผมกำลังเรียนภาษาไทย
I am learning the Thai language

นี่คืออีเมลของผม
Here is my email address:
Tommy_atkins@defdomain.net

ด้วยความนับถือ
Regards

ทอมมี่
Tommy

"จดหมายอะไรครับ"
"What does it say?"

"ฉันไม่รู้ค่ะ ถามแพนเค้กกันเถอะ"
"I don't know, let's ask Pancake"

ค ควาย

 Water Buffalo

"ส-วัส-ดี ค่ะ แพน-เค้ก, คุณ อ่าน จด-หมาย นี้ ได้ ไหม"

"sà-wàt-dii kâ pεεn-kéek, kun àan jòt-măai níi dâi măi?"

"เสีย-ใจ ครับ, ผม อ่าน ไม่ ได้"

"sĭia-jai kráp, pŏm àan man mâi dâi."

"ผู้-หญิง ที่ บ้าน นั้น อาจ-จะ อ่าน ได้"

"pûu-yĭng tîi bâan nán àat-jà àan dâi."

"เป็น ความ คิด ที่ ดี ขอบ-คุณ ค่ะ"

"bpen kwaam kít tîi dii kɔ̀ɔp-kun kâ."

Question?

Instead of question marks (?), Thai uses a number of *question particles*, including ไหม (măi).

A reply to a *măi* question is made by repeating the verb if the answer is 'yes', or using ไม่ + **the verb** if the answer is 'no'. Pancake literally replies, "*I read cannot*," (*pŏm àan mâi dâi*).

Consonant Sound: /k/

4th Letter of the Alphabet   Kɔɔ Kwaai

คือ (kʉʉ – *[to] be*); เคย (kəəi – *use to*); นาค (nâak - *serpent*)

๗ คน   Person

Thai Culture - Respect

Showing respect is a huge cultural element of Thai life. Conversely, not showing respect will mark you as someone who either doesn't know or simply rude.

This respect can be from simple things like taking your shoes off before you enter someone's home, to how you address another person, or the way you dress.

We will cover some of these to ensure you get the most out of your time in the LOS.

This Consonant is Obsolete.

5th Letter of the Alphabet   Kɔɔ Kon

ฆ ระฆัง Bell

"คุณ พ่อ คะ, พี่ คะ, อา-หาร พร้อม แล้ว ค่ะ"
"kun pɔ̂ɔ ká, pîi ká, aa-hǎan prɔ́ɔm lɛ́ɛɔ kâ"

Thai Culture - The Head and the Feet

The head is the highest point on the body and Thais believe it to be spiritually above everything else. *Never* touch anyone on the head without asking their permission first, this also applies to children.

It is also considered rude to pass in the space above someone's head if they are sitting or kneeling.

You will see Thai people bow or crouch as they walk past you if you are sitting, this is to show respect. It would be very polite of you to do the same if you find yourself in a similar situation.

Consonant Sound: /k/

Kɔɔ Rá-kang

"คุณพ่อคะ พี่คะ อาหารพร้อมแล้วค่ะ"

"Father, brother, food is ready."

Thai Culture - The Head and the Feet

The feet are the lowest part and are considered dirty. *Always* take your shoes off when entering someone's home. Never point your feet at other people and always walk around another's outstretched legs.

All Thai currency has His Majesty the King's portrait on it, if you drop a note, *never* step on it!

ฆ-รา-วาส (ká-raa-wâat – *buddhist layperson*); เมฆ (mêek – *cloud*)

68

ง ง งู Snake

Thai Culture - Nicknames

For a westerner, Thai names can be a little bit difficult to get your tongue around. Fortunately, just about every Thai person has a nickname (*chûu-lêen*, ชื่อ-เล่น).

This is given to them by their parents at birth and is used throughout their life.

Consonant Sound: /ng/

7th Letter of the Alphabet — Ngɔɔ Nguu

[หาว] "หิวมาก"
[Yawn] "I'm very hungry!"

"ไอยาราอยู่ที่ไหน เขาจะต้องหิวแน่นอน"
"Where is Aiyarah, he'll be hungry."

Some of these nicknames can be humorous to foreigners but these are just friendly names. The fact that the person's name translates as chicken, frog, or duck may give you a chuckle but you'll get over it.

Increasingly, due to Western influences, more and more Thais are being given English names.

ง่าย (ngâai – *easy*); เงิน (ngəən – *money*); แกง (gɛɛng – *curry*)

จ จาน   Plate

"กิน กัน เถอะ"
"gin gan tà"

"ลูก-ชาย, ดน-ตรี โรง-เรียน ของ-ลูก เริ่ม กี่ โมง"
"lûuk-chaai, don-dtrii roong-riian kɔ̌ɔng-lûuk rə̂əm gìi moong"

"บ่าย 2 โมง ตรง ครับ"
"bàai sɔ̌ɔng moong dtrong kráp"

Thai Family Terms

- ผู้-ชาย (pûu-chaai - *man*)
- ผู้-หญิง (pûu-yǐng - *woman*)
- ผู้-ใหญ่ (pûu-yài - *adult*)
- เด็ก (dèk - *child*)
- ลูก-ชาย (lûuk-chaai - *son*)
- ลูก-สาว (lûuk-sǎao - *daughter*)
- สา-มี (sǎa-mii - *husband*)
- ภรร-ยา (pan-rá-yaa - *wife*)
- พ่อ (pɔ̂ɔ - *father*)
- แม่ (mɛ̂ɛ - *mother*)

Initial Consonant Sound: /j/ Final Consonant Sound: /t/

8th Letter of the Alphabet   Jɔɔ Jaan

"กิน กันเถอะ"
"Let's eat."

"ลูกชาย,ดนตรีโรงเรียนของลูก เริ่มกี่โมง"
"Son, what time does your school concert start?"

"บ่าย 2 โมงตรงครับ"
"At 2 p.m"

Thai Family Terms (continued)

- ผัว (pǔa - *husband* (informal))
- เมีย (miia - *wife* (informal))
- พี่-น้อง (pîi-nɔ́ɔng - *relative*)
- พี่-ชาย (pîi-chaai - *older brother*)
- พี่-สาว (pîi-sǎao - *older sister*)
- น้อง-ชาย (nɔ́ɔng-chaai - *younger brother*)
- น้อง-สาว (nɔ́ɔng-sǎao - *younger sister*)
- ปู่ (bpùu - *father's father*)
- ย่า (yâa - *father's mother*)
- more to follow...

จริง (jing – *really, true*); จาก (jàak – *from*); ใจ (jai – *heart*); ธุ-ร-กิจ (tú-rá-gìt – *business*)

ฉ ฉิ่ง   Cymbals

"ปี ที่ แล้ว เดิน ข-บวน ส-นุก มาก ครับ"
"bpii tîi lέεo dəən kà-buan sà-nùk mâak kráp"

"พ่อ คิด ว่า วัน-นี้ ฝน จะ ตก"
"pɔ̂ɔ kít wâa wan-níi fŏn jà dtòk"

"แม่ จะ เอา ร่ม ไป ด้วย"
"mɛ̂ɛ jà ao rôm bpai dûai"

Thai Family Terms (contd)
- ตา (dtaa - *mother's father*)
- ยาย (yaai - *mother's mother*)
- ลุง (lung - *father/mother's older brother*)
- ป้า (bpâa - *father/mother's older sister*)
- น้า (náa - *mother's younger brother or sister*)
- อา (aa - *father's younger brother or sister*).

Initial Consonant Sound: /ch/ Final Consonant Sound: /t/

Note: the actual cymbals denoted by the Thai word 'chìng' are only small, they have been enlarged here for illustrative purposes.

ฉัน (chǎn – [female]: *I, me* (informal)); ฉ-ลาด (chà-làat – *clever*)

ช ช้าง

 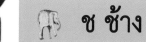 Elephant

Thai Culture - the Wai

The Wai is used to greet and show respect to people. This is where one's hands are joined as if in prayer and then a bow of the head is given to the person you are greeting or showing respect to.

The height of the hands and the depth of the bow indicate one's social status in reference to the other person, i.e. the person of lower social standing will Wai first, their hands will be positioned higher, and their bow will be deeper than the reciprocated Wai.

Adults do not normally Wai to children (though children will Wai to adults).

Initial Consonant Sound: /ch/ Final Consonant Sound: /t/

You must always show respect and Wai with your hands 'high' to monks and it shows great respect to Wai to older Thai people.

You should never Wai to service people such as waiters or bar staff.

There are 5 levels/heights of Wai but if, initially, you Wai with your fingertips touching the tip of your nose you won't go far wrong.

ชาย (chaai – *male*); ใช้ (chái – *use*); เอก-ราช (èek-gà-râat – *independence*)

ซ โซ่

Chain

Initial Consonant Sound: /s/ Final Consonant Sound: /t/

11th Letter of the Alphabet Sɔɔ Sôo

ซ้าย (sáai – *left*); ซื้อ (sʉʉ – *buy*); ก๊าซ (gáat – *gas*)

ฌ

 ฌ เฌอ Tree

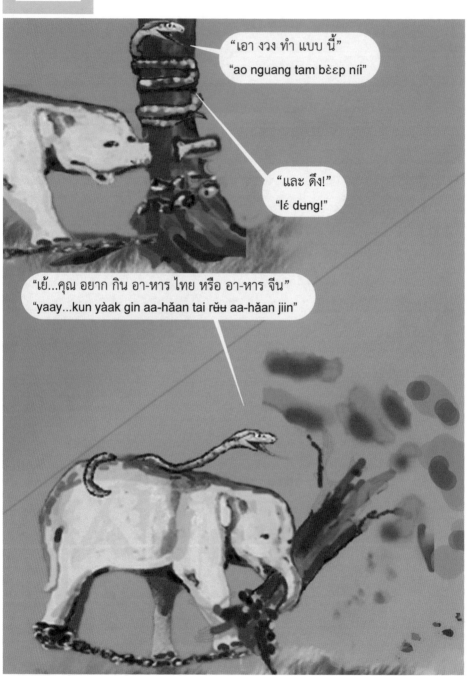

Initial Consonant Sound: /ch/ Final Consonant Sound: /t/

Chɔɔ Chəə

Surin Elephant Festival

The elephant is held in great esteem in Thailand and the Surin Elephant Festival takes place on the third Saturday in November.

Here hundreds of elephants show their skills and play tug-of-war, football, dance and perform.

It is a great event, attended by people from all across the country and foreigners alike, and is well worth a visit.

ฌาน (chaan – *contemplation*, e.g. เข้า ฌาน (kâo chaan – *meditate*))

ญ

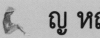 ญ หญิง Woman

Initial Consonant Sound: /y/ Final Consonant Sound: /n/

13th Letter of the Alphabet   Yɔɔ Yĭng ญ

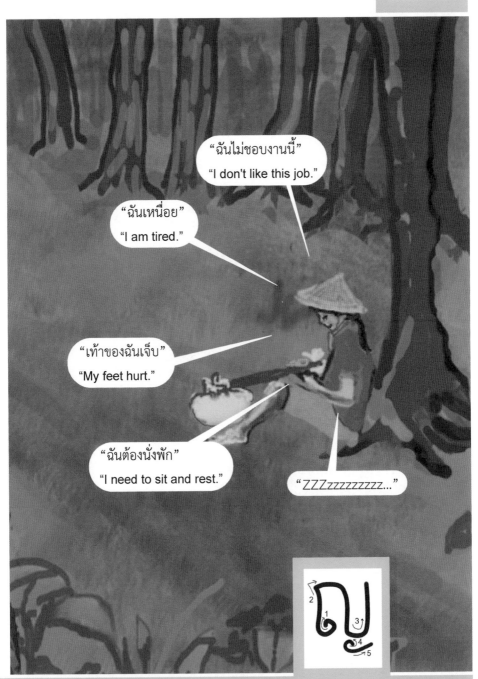

ญาติ (yâat – *relations*, *kin*, *cousin*), ผลาญ (plăan – *destroy*, *ruin*, *waste*)

ฎ ชฎา

Head-dress

"ฉัน อยาก เป็น นาง-รำ"

"chăn yàak bpen naang-ram"

"หรือ ฉัน อาจ-จะ สา-มารถ ช่วย ปก-ป้อง ประ-เทศ ของ ฉัน"

"rǔu chăn àat-jà săa-mâat chûuai bpòk-bpɔ̂ɔng bprà-têet kɔ̌ɔng chăn"

Thai Culture - Anthems

The Thai royal family hold a special place in the heart of all Thais and, while in Thailand, you will undoubtedly hear the royal anthem being played. When you do, please stand and show your respect at this time.

The National Anthem is played twice daily at 0800 and 1800 at which time everyone stops what they are doing, stand to attention and pay respect to the anthem.

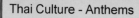

Initial Consonant Sound: /d/ Final Consonant Sound: /t/

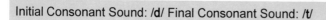

14th Letter of the Alphabet   Dɔɔ Chá-daa

ชฎา (chá-daa - *head-dress*); ฎี-กา (dii-gaa – *supreme court*); กฎ (gòt – *rule*)

ฏ ปฏัก — Spear

"ฉัน ต้อง-การ เป็น นัก-รบ"
"chǎn dtɔ̂ɔng-gaan bpen nák-róp"

"และ เข้ม-แข็ง"
"lɛ́ kêem-kɛ̌ng"

- Day - *wan* (วัน) / Night - *kʉʉn* (คืน)
- Today - *wan-níi* (วัน-นี้)
- Tomorrow - *prûng-níi* (พรุ่ง-นี้)
- After tomorrow - *má-rʉʉn-níi* (มะ-รืน-นี้)
- Yesterday - *mʉ̂a-waan-níi* (เมื่อ-วาน-นี้)
- Before yesterday - *mʉ̂a-waan-sʉʉn* (เมื่อ-วาน-ซีน)
- Week - *aa-tít* (อา-ทิตย์) or sàp-daa (สับ-ดาห์)
- Weekend - *sǎo aa-tít* (เสาร์ อา-ทิตย์)

Initial Consonant Sound: **/dt/** Final Consonant Sound: **/t/**

15th Letter of the Alphabet   Dtɔɔ Bpà-dtàk

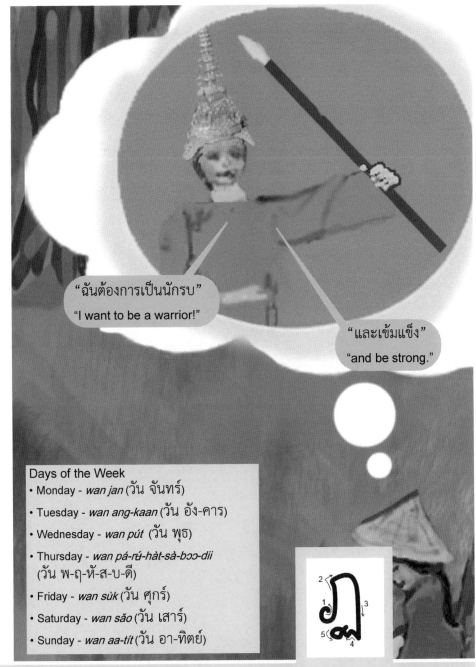

"ฉันต้องการเป็นนักรบ"
"I want to be a warrior!"

"และเข้มแข็ง"
"and be strong."

Days of the Week
• Monday - *wan jan* (วัน จันทร์)
• Tuesday - *wan ang-kaan* (วัน อัง-คาร)
• Wednesday - *wan pút* (วัน พุธ)
• Thursday - *wan pá-rʉ́-hàt-sà-bɔɔ-dii*
(วัน พ-ฤ-หั-ส-บ-ดี)
• Friday - *wan sùk* (วัน ศุกร์)
• Saturday - *wan săo* (วัน เสาร์)
• Sunday - *wan aa-tít* (วัน อา-ทิตย์)

ป-ฏิ-ทิน (bpà-dtì-tin – *calendar*); ปรา-กฏ (bpràa-gòt – *appear*)

 ฐ ฐาน   Pedestal

"ฉัน จะ นำ กอง-ทัพ"

"chǎn jà nam gɔɔng-táp..."

"และ ปราบ ศัต-รู ทั้ง-หมด"

"...lɛ́ bpràap sàt-dtruu táng-mòt"

Thai Culture - Muay Thai

Most people have heard of Muay Thai, or Thai boxing. It is the traditional martial art in Thailand and most towns and cities will host competitions on a regular basis.

Before the bout, the *Wâi kruu ram muai* ceremony (ไหว้ ครู รำ มวย), is performed in the ring. This is an ancient ritual where the combatants pay their respects to their teachers and elders.

On completion, their ceremonial headbands are removed and the first of up to five, 3-minute rounds commences.

Fists, knees, hands, elbows and feet may be used and any part of the body, except the groin, may be hit.

Points are scored for every hit and penalty points are deducted for violations.

The competition ends with either a physical or a technical knockout, by the referees decision, or in a draw.

Source: http://www.muaythai-fighting.com

Consonant Sound: /t/

Tɔ̌ɔ Tăan

ฐา-นะ (tăa-ná - *status, position*); ฐาน (tăan – *base*); อิฐ (it – *brick*)

ฑ ฑ มณโฑ

Giant's Wife

"ให้ ปี-ศาจ ช่วย พวก-เรา"
"hâi bpii-sàat chûai pûuak rao"

"และ...เดี๋ยว-ก่อน, คุณ ไม่ ใช่ ปี-ศาจ"
"lέ...dǐiao-gɔ̀ɔn, kun mâi châi bpii-sàat?"

Thai Culture - The Story of Nang Montoo

In Thai literature, a fox resides with 4 Rɯɯ-sǐis (ฤๅ-ษี - *hermit sages*) who give the fox food.

One day, a serpent-demon (nâak (นาค)), who was once embarassed by the Rɯɯ-sǐis, releases her poison into some milk in an effort to kill the sages.

The fox sees this and as it can't speak it jumps into the milk to protect the Rɯɯ-sǐis. The fox drinks the milk and dies.

In gratitude, Rɯɯ-sǐi uses his magic to transform the dead fox into a beautiful lady and then escorts her to an angel in heaven.

Later, as a prize for straightening a mountain, the angel gives Nang Montoo to a giant to become his beautiful wife.

Tɔɔ Mon-too

มณ-ฑล (mon-ton – *county, precinct, circle*); ครุฑ (krút – *garuda (a mythical bird)*)

ตม

ตม ผู้เฒ่า — Elderly Man

Thai Culture - Saving Face

Saving face is a huge factor in understanding Thai people and their culture.

Many people are sensitive to this concept and Thai people are no exception: no one wants to be seen to lose face.

Very often an uncomfortable situation will be treated with a smile and the uttering of *mâi bpen rai* (ไม่ เป็น ไร): this often used phrase typifies Thai attitude and it basically means never mind, it'll be okay; somewhat similar to the French c'est la vie.

Consonant Sound: /t/

Tɔɔ Pûu-tâo

เต่า (tâo - *elderly, old*); อัฒจันทร์ (àt-tá-jan - *grandstand stand*)

ณ

 ณ เณร   Monk

"ไม่ มี ความ จำ-เป็น ที่ จะ สู้-รบ"
"mâi mii kwaam jam-bpen tîi jà sûu-róp"

"คิด-ถึง กรรม ดี"
"kít-tǔng gam dii"

Thai Culture - Buddhism

Thailand is approximately 95% Theravada Buddhist and is strongly influenced by traditional beliefs regarding ancestral and natural spirits which have been incorporated into Buddhist cosmology.

Most Thai people own spirit houses, miniature wooden houses in which they believe household spirits live. They present offerings of food and drink to these spirits to keep them happy. If these spirits aren't happy, it is believed that they will inhabit the larger household of the Thai and cause chaos. These spirit houses can be found in public places and in the streets of Thailand, where the public make offerings.

Source: www.en.wikipedia.org/wiki/Culture_of_Thailand

Consonant Sound: /n/

Nɔɔ Neen

ณ เว-ลา นั้น (ná wee-laa nán - *at that time*); ประ-มาณ (bprá-maan - *about*)

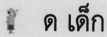 ด เด็ก　　　Child

20th Letter of the Alphabet   Dɔɔ Dèk

ดู (duu – *look*); เดิน (dəən – *walk*); ได้ (dâi – *can, able*); วาด (wâat – *draw*)

ต

 ต เต่า   Turtle

Thai Culture - Temples

Most temples have a dress code. This usually means shoulders must be covered and in some temples, long trousers are required.

You must always remove your shoes before you enter the sacred areas of a temple. You will see where to leave your shoes, they are quite safe.

When you sit or kneel within the temple, be careful not to point your feet at a Buddha image or anything that is sacred, tuck your feet away.

Initial Consonant Sound: **/dt/** Final Consonant Sound: **/t/**

21st Letter of the Alphabet　　　Dtɔɔ Dtào 　

Photography is permitted within temples unless signs say otherwise.

Before you begin taking photographs, please show respect to the temple, to Buddha and to a monk if one is present. I have seen too many tourists enter a temple and just start clicking away!

It is also polite to show respect as you leave.

แต่ (dtɛ̀ɛ – *but, since*); ต-ลก (dtà-lòk – *funny*); อนุญาต (à-nú-yâat- *permit*)

ถ ถุง   Bag

ถึง (tŭng - *reach, arrive*); ถาม (tăam – *ask*); สามารถ (să-mâat – *can, be able to*)

ท

 ท ทหาร   Soldier

Consonant Sound: /t/

23rd Letter of the Alphabet ผ Tɔɔ Tá-hǎan

ทอด (tɔ̂ɔd – *deep-fried*); ทำไม (tam-mai – *why*); ปราสาท (bpraa-sàat – *castle*)

ธ ธง   Flag

Consonant Sound: /t/

24th Letter of the Alphabet Tɔɔ Tong

ธรรม (tham – *dharma, religious teaching/duty*); โกรธ (gròot – *angry*)

น

 น หนู   Mouse

"เช้า นี้ ยุ่ง มาก!"
"cháo níi yûng maak"

"ผม ต้อง ไป พบ เพื่อน ของ ผม"
"pǒm dtɔ̂ɔng bpai póp pûuan kɔ̌ɔng pǒm"

"ผม จะ ใช้ ใบ ไหน ดี"
"pǒm jà chái bai nǎi dii"

Thai Culture - Monks

Monks have a special status in Thailand and are respected throughout society.

Monks and laymen follow the *Vinaya* - prá-wí-nai (พระ-วิ-นัย). This is the framework for the education and discipline for Buddhism.

At the core of the *Vinaya* are the rules known as *Precepts*. These are the directives that monks live their lives by and will lead them to greater wisdow. There are different levels of Precepts, 5 for the majority of buddhists, 8 and 10 for laymen, and 227 Precepts for ordained monks (Bhikkus (pík-kù, ภิก-ขุ)).

Source: http://siamfoundation.org/thailand-faq/index.php?action=artikel&cat=5&id=3&artlang=en

Consonant Sound: /n/

25th Letter of the Alphabet   Nɔɔ Nǔn

นม (nom – *milk*); นก (nók – *bird*); นั่ง (nâng – *sit*); นั้น (nán – *that*)

บ

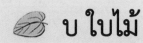 บ ใบไม้

Leaf

"วัน-นี้ อา-กาศ ดี"

"wan-níi aa-gàat dii"

"จะ ใช้ ใบ นี้"

"jà chái bai níi"

"โอ-เว่น อยู่ ที่-ไหน"

"Oo-wêen yùu tîi-nǎi"

Thai Culture - Religious Merit

Many Thai's support monks with donations of food and other similar acts of aid. This brings them religious merit or bun (บุญ) which will assist them in this and in the next life.

If you got to a temple and a monk wants to practice his English then it is okay to talk to him.

Remember, always keep your head lower than his and if you wish to give him something, place it on the ground in front of him.

Women must never touch a monk or a monk's robe and must never sit next to a monk unless it is at a lower level.

Initial Consonant Sound: **/b/** Final Consonant Sound: **/p/**

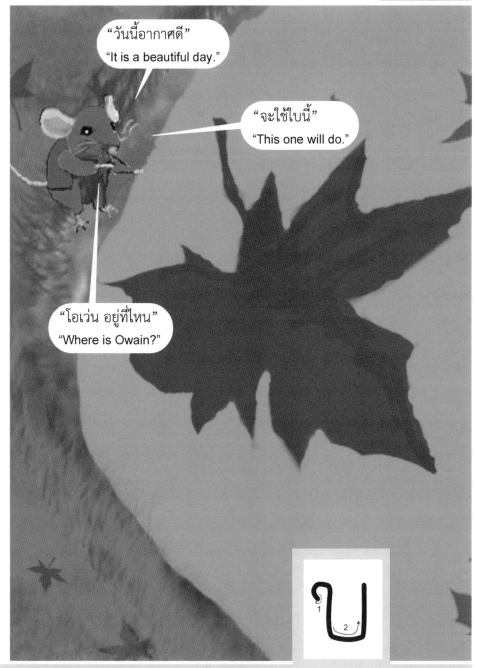

บ้าน (bâan – *house, home*); พบ (póp – *meet, find*)

ป

🔊 ป ปลา　　　　　Fish

"ส-วัส-ดี ครับ เอล-โม่, คุณ ได้ ลูก-กวาด ของ ผม ไหม"
"sà-wàt-dii kráp eel-môo, kun dâi lûuk-gwàat kɔ̌ɔng pǒm mǎi"

"ครับ, นี่ ไง"
"kráp, nîi ngai"

"ขอบ-คุณ ครับ เอล-โม่, เจอ กัน พรุ่ง-นี้ ครับ"
"kɔ̀ɔp-kun kráp eel-môo, jəə gan prûng-níi kráp"

"ตก-ลง ครับ"
"dtòk-long kráp"

Initial Consonant Sound: **/bp/** Final Consonant Sound: **/p/**

27th Letter of the Alphabet   Bpɔɔ Bplaa

ปี (bpii – *year*); เปิด (bpə̀ət – *open*); ปิด (bpìt – *close*); สัป-ดาห์ (sàp-daa – *week*)

ผ ผึ้ง   Bee

"พวก เขา อยู่ ที่-ไหน"
"pûuak kǎo yùu tîi-nǎi"

"พวก เขา อยู่ ที่-นี่ ที่-ใด ที่-หนึ่ง"
"pûuak kǎo yùu tîi-nîi tîi-dai tîi-nɯ̀ng"

Thai Culture - Buddhist Precepts

The **Five Precepts** are the basic guidelines for all buddhists:

1. To refrain from destroying living creatures

2. To refrain from stealing

3. To refrain from adulterous, or wrong sexual activity

4. To refrain from lying, slanderous or harmful speech

5. To refrain from intoxicating drinks and drugs which lead to carelessness.

Remember, these are guidelines not rules, and not everyone sticks to them.

Source: http://siamfoundation.org/thailand-faq/index.php?action=artikel&cat=5&id=3&artlang=en

Consonant Sound: **/p/**

28th letter of the Alphabet   Pɔ̌ɔ Pûng

"พวกเขาอยู่ที่ไหน"
"Where are they?"

"พวกเขาอยู่ที่นี่ที่ใดที่หนึ่ง"
"They are here somewhere."

10 Precepts:

6. To refrain from eating after mid-day
7. To refrain from dancing, singing, music, going to see entertainments,
8. To refrain from wearing garlands, using perfumes, and beautifying the body with cosmetics
9. To refrain from lying on a high or luxurious sleeping place
10. To refrain from accepting gold and silver (money).

ผิด (pìt – *wrong, incorrect*); ผ่าน (pàan – *cross, pass*); แผ่น (pὲεn – *sheet, plank*)

ฝ ฝา   Lid

"พวก-เขา อยู่ ที่-นั่น"
"pûuak-kăo yùu tîi-nân"

"งาน-เลี้ยง ได้ เริ่ม แล้ว"
"ngaan-líiang dâi rôəm lɛ́ɛo"

"ฝา สวย!"
"făa sŭai"

Months of the Year

January - *má-gà-raa-kom* (ม-ก-รา-คม)	July - *gà-rá-gà-daa-kom* (ก-ร-ก-ฏา-คม)
February - *gum-paa-pan* (กุม-ภา-พันธ์)	August - *sĭng-hăa-kom* (สิง-หา-คม)
March - *mii-naa-kom* (มี-นา-คม)	September - *gan-yaa-yon* (กัน-ยา-ยน)
April - *mee-săa-yon* (เม-ษา-ยน)	October - *dtù-laa-kom* (ตุ-ลา-คม)
May - *prút-sà-paa-kom* (พฤ-ษ-ภา-คม)	November - *prút-sà-jì-gaa-yon* (พฤ-ศ-จิ-กา-ยน)
June - *mí-tù-naa-yon* (มิ-ถุ-นา-ยน)	December - *tan-waa-kom* (ธัน-วา-คม)

Fǒ̌w Fǎa

ฝน (fǒn – *rain*); ฝรั่ง (fà-ràng – *non-Asian foreigner*); ฝัน (fǎn – *dream*)

พ พาน   Tray

Consonant Sound: **/p/**

30th Letter of the Alphabet   Pɔɔ Paan

พี่ (pīi - *older sibling*); เพิ่ง (pə̂əng - *just now, recent*); ภาพ (pâap - *picture*)

ฟ

ฟ ฟัน   Tooth

Eating Out

In Thailand, eating out with friends is a popular occurrence and a great social occasion: it's all part of the concept of *sà-nùk* (สนุก).

When you sit to eat, there is no starter and main course, everybody orders and the food is set down for all to enjoy.

The waiter or waitress will serve you your plate with just rice or in a bowl.

Initial Consonant Sound: /f/ Final Consonant Sound: /p/

Fɔɔ Fan

Use the serving spoon with each dish to bring food to your plate, no more than one or two spoonfulls at a time and then savour the delcious textures, flavours and spices with cooked rice (kâao sŭai, ข้าว สวย).

ไฟ (fai – *fire, flame*); ฟ้า (fáa – *sky*); ฟัง (fang – *listen*); กราฟ (gràap – *graph*)

ภ

 ภ สำเภา   Junk

Songkran

The three day Songkran festival (Sŏng-graan - สง-กรานต์) marks the start of the Thai New Year. It runs from 13-15th April and is a national holiday.

The festival involves sprinkling water onto holy images in order to cleanse and in hope that it will bring good luck and prosperity in the forthcoming year.

Consonant Sound: /p/

Nowadays though, for a lot of people, the emphasis is more towards partying, soaking people, and covering them in chalk (*din-sɔ̆ɔ-pɔɔng* - ดิน-สอ-พอง).

ภา-ษา (paa-săa – *language*, *speech*, *words*); ลาภ (lâap – *luck, fortune*)

ม

 ม ม้า — Horse

Mɔɔ Máa

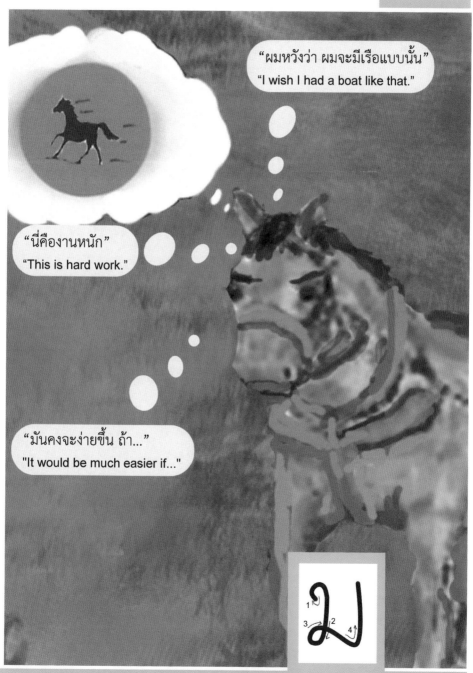

มาก (mâak – *much, many*); ไม่ (mâi – *no, not*); เมีย (miia – *wife*); จาม (jaam - *sneeze*)

ย

 ย ยักษ์ Giant

"...ยักษ์ ช่วย ผม"
"...yák chûai pŏm"

"จาก นั้น ผม คง จะ ดึง เรือ นี้ อย่าง ง่าย ๆ"
"jàak nán pŏm kong jà dɯng rɯɯa níi yàang ngâai ngâai"

Initial Consonant Sound: /y/ Final Consonant Sound: /i/

34th Letter of the Alphabet   Yɔɔ Yák

" ...ยักษ์ช่วยผม "

"...a giant helped me!"

" จากนั้น ผมคงจะดึงเรือนี้อย่างง่าย ๆ "

"Then I could pull this boat easily."

ยาก (yâak – *hard, difficult*); ยัง (yang – *yet, still*); ง่าย (ngâai - *easy*)

ร

 ร เรือ   Boat

Initial Consonant Sound: /r/ Final Consonant Sound: /n/

125

Rɔɔ Rʉʉa ร

เร็ว (reo – *fast, quick*); รำ (ram – *dance*); เรียก (rîiak – *call*); พร (pɔɔn – *blessing*)

ล ล ลิง

Monkey

Initial Consonant Sound: /l/ Final Consonant Sound: /n/

36th Letter of the Alphabet Lɔɔ Ling

ลืม (lɯɯm – *forget*); เล่น (lêen – *play, have fun, amuse*); กล (gon - *trickery*)

ว

ว แหวน   Ring

Initial Consonant Sound: /w/ Final Consonant Sound: /o/

Wɔɔ Wɛ̌ɛn 💍 ว

เวลา (wee-laa – *time*); วัด (wât - *temple, measure*); แก้ว (gɛ̂ɛo - glass)

 ศ ศาลา   Tent/Pavilion

Initial Consonant Sound: /s/ Final Consonant Sound: /t/

131

ศูนย์ (sǔun – *zero, 0*); ศาล (sǎan – *court*); อากาศ (aa-gàat – *weather*)

ษ ฤๅษี   Hermit

"ขอ-โทษ ครับ ท่าน ฤๅ-ษี"
"kɔ̌ɔ-tôot kráp tâan rɯɯ-sǐi"

"มี อะ-ไร ให้ ช่วย ไหม"
"mii à-rai hâi chûuai mǎi"

"ผม เก็บ แหวน นี้ ได้ และ อยาก คืน มัน ให้ เจ้า-ของ ครับ"
"pǒm gèp wɛ̌ɛn níi dâi lɛ́ yàak kɯɯn man hâi jâo-kɔ̌ɔng kráp"

"ทิ้ง มัน ไว้ ที่ นี่ เจ้า-ของ มัน จะ มา รับ คืน"
"tíng man wái tîi nîi jâo-kɔ̌ɔng man jà maa ráp kɯɯn"

Initial Consonant Sound: /s/ Final Consonant Sound: /t/

ฤๅ Ruu-sǐi

"ขอโทษครับ ท่านฤๅษี"
"Excuse me ruu-sǐi?"

มีอะไรให้ช่วยไหม"
"How can I help you."

"ผมเก็บแหวนนี้ได้และอยากคืนมันให้เจ้าของครับ"
"I have found this beautiful ring and want to return it to its owner."

"ทิ้งมันไว้ที่นี่เจ้าของมันจะมารับคืน"
"Leave it here, its owner will receive it. "

ภา-ษา ไทย (paa-sǎa tai - *Thai Language*); กระ-ดาษ (grà-dàat - *paper*)

ส

 ส เสือ　　　　Tiger

Initial Consonant Sound: **/s/** Final Consonant Sound: **/t/**

สิง-โต (sĭng-dto – *lion*); ใส่ (sài – *add, put in*); โอ-กาส (oo-gàat – *opportunity chance*)

ห

ห หีบ   Chest

Consonant Sound: /h/ (Can also be a silent consonant: /-/)

Hŏɔ Hìip

หก (hòk - *six, 6*); หนัง (năng - *movie, leather*); หมด (mòt - *empty, finish*)

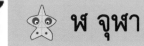 ฬ จุฬา   Star-shaped Kite

Initial Consonant Sound: /l/ Final Consonant Sound: /n/

Lɔɔ Jù-laa

จุ-ฬา (jù-laa – *star* or *bird shaped kite*); ปลา-วาฬ (bplaa-waan – *whale*)

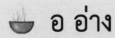

อ อ่าง   Bowl

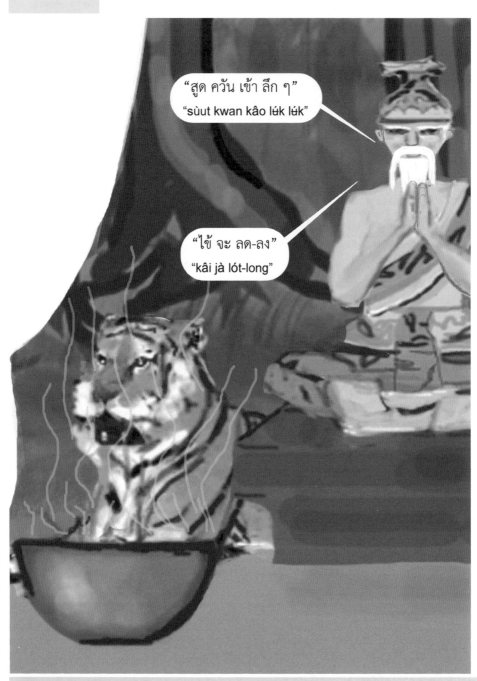

Consonant Sound: /ɔɔ/ (Can also be a silent consonant: /-/)

43rd Letter of the Alphabet ʋ Àang

อัง-กฤษ (ang-grìt - *English*); อยู่ (yùu – *[to be] somewhere (location)*); ขอ (kɔ̌ɔ - *request*)

ฮ ฮ นกฮูก   Owl

44th Letter of the Alphabet   Hɔɔ Nók-hûuk

ฮึก-เหิม (húk-hɤ̌ɤm - *arrogant, conceited*); ฮ่อง-กง (*Hɔ̂ɔng-Kong - Hong Kong*)

Appendix

Appendix A. Initial and Final Consonant Sounds

The table below shows a complete list of consonants colour coded by consonant class, their initial and their final consonant sounds:

Table A.1 - Initial and Final Consonant Sounds

No.	Thai Character	Transliterated Text Name	Meaning	Initial Consonant Sound	Final Consonant Sound
1	ก ไก่	Gɔɔ Gài	Chicken	/g/	/k/
2	ข ไข่	Kɔ̌ɔ Kài	Egg	/k/	
3	ฃ ขวด	Kɔ̌ɔ Kùuat	Bottle	Obsolete	
4	ค ควาย	Kɔɔ Kwaai	Buffalo	/k/	
5	ฅ คน	Kɔɔ Kon	Person	Obsolete	
6	ฆ ระฆัง	Kɔɔ Rá-kang	Bell	/k/	
7	ง งู	Ngɔɔ Nguu	Snake	/ng/	
8	จ จาน	Jɔɔ Jaan	Plate	/j/	/t/
9	ฉ ฉิ่ง	Chɔ̌ɔ Chìng	Cymbals	/ch/	/t/
10	ช ช้าง	Chɔɔ Cháang	Elephant	/ch/	/t/
11	ซ โซ่	Sɔɔ Sôo	Chain	/s/	/t/
12	ฌ เฌอ	Chɔɔ Chəə	Tree	/ch/	/t/
13	ญ หญิง	Yɔɔ Yǐng	Woman	/y/	/n/
14	ฎ ชฎา	Dɔɔ Chá-daa	Head-dress	/d/	/t/
15	ฏ ปฏัก	Dtɔɔ Bpà-dtàk	Spear	/dt/	/t/
16	ฐ ฐาน	Tɔ̌ɔ Tǎan	Pedestal	/t/	
17	ฑ มณโท	Tɔɔ Mon-too	Giant's Wife	/t/	
18	ฒ ผู้เฒ่า	Tɔɔ Pûu-tâo	Old Man	/t/	
19	ณ เณร	Nɔɔ Neen	Monk	/n/	
20	ด เด็ก	Dɔɔ Dèk	Child	/d/	/t/

Table A.1 - Initial and Final Consonant Sounds

21	ต เต่า	Dtɔɔ Dtào	Turtle	/dt/	/t/
22	ถ ถุง	Tɔɔ Tŭng	Bag	/t/	
23	ท ทหาร	Tɔɔ Tá-hǎan	Soldier	/t/	
24	ธ ธง	Tɔɔ Tong	Flag	/t/	
25	น หนู	Nɔɔ Nǔu	Mouse	/n/	
26	บ ใบไม้	Bɔɔ Bai-mái	Leaf	/b/	/p/
27	ป ปลา	Bpɔɔ Bplaa	Fish	/bp/	/p/
28	ผ ผึ้ง	Pɔɔ Pûng	Bee	/p/	
29	ฝ ฝา	Fɔɔ Fǎa	Lid	/f/	/p/
30	พ พาน	Pɔɔ Paan	Tray	/p/	
31	ฟ ฟัน	Fɔɔ Fan	Tooth	/f/	/p/
32	ภ สำเภา	Pɔɔ Sǎm-pao	Junk	/p/	
33	ม ม้า	Mɔɔ Máa	Horse	/m/	
34	ย ยักษ์	Yɔɔ Yák	Giant	/y/	/i/
35	ร เรือ	Rɔɔ Rʉʉa	Boat	/r/	/n/
36	ล ลิง	Lɔɔ Ling	Monkey	/l/	/n/
37	ว แหวน	Wɔɔ Wɛ̌ɛn	Ring	/w/	/o/
38	ศ ศาลา	Sɔɔ Sǎa-laa	Tent	/s/	/t/
39	ษ ฤๅษี	Sɔɔ Rʉʉ-sǐi	Hermit	/s/	/t/
40	ส เสือ	Sɔɔ Sʉ̌ʉa	Tiger	/s/	/t/
41	ห หีบ	Hɔɔ Hìip	Chest	/h/	
42	ฬ จุฬา	Lɔɔ Jù-laa	Star-shaped Kite	/l/	/n/
43	อ อ่าง	ɔɔ Àang	Bowl	/ɔɔ/	
44	ฮ นกฮูก	Hɔɔ Nók-hûuk	Owl	/h/	

Appendix B. Summary of the Alphabet Story

The following list is a summary of the entire 44 consonant story. Learning this will help to recall the story, remind you of the individual consonant names, and the sequence of the alphabet.

1. Millie (มิลลี่), the <u>chicken</u>, says hello.
2. Millie goes to meet her <u>egg</u>-friend Pollo (พอลโล่), who has found a bottle.
3. They try to read the message (in a <u>bottle</u>). They can't, so they ask Pancake.
4. They ask Pancake (แพนเค้ก) the <u>water buffalo</u> if he can read it; he can't so suggests asking the woman in the house.
5. Mother (<u>person</u>) is cooking lunch for her daughter.
6. The daughter rings the <u>bell</u> for food.
7. This wakes Ashara (อาชารา) the <u>snake</u> who goes to find Aiyarah.
8. The family sits for dinner and mother passes the <u>plates</u>.
9. The son gets his <u>cymbals</u> for the school parade.
10. Ashara finds Aiyarah (ไอยารา) the <u>elephant</u>.
11. Aiyarah is attached to the tree with a <u>chain</u>.
12. Aiyarah and Ashara, pull the <u>tree</u> out.
13. <u>Woman</u> rests in a clearing and falls asleep. She then starts to dream.
14. Perhaps she will be a famous dancer (dons her <u>head-dress</u>).
15. Then she picks up a <u>spear</u>.
16. Whilst standing on a <u>pedestal</u>, she addresses her army.
17. She then tries to summon a demon but Nang Montoo, the <u>giant's wife</u>, appears to calm her down.
18. Then her father, now an <u>elderly man</u>, appears in her dream.
19. Finally, a young <u>monk</u> talks to her through her dream.
20. Then she is woken by her <u>child</u>, who needs help.
21. They see a wounded <u>turtle</u>.
22. She has medicine in her <u>bag</u> and helps the turtle.
23. A company of <u>soldiers</u> marches past...
24. ...carrying their Thai <u>flag</u>.
25. A <u>mouse</u>, Elmo (เอลโม่), watches this from the river bank...

26. ...and gets on a <u>leaf</u> to go and see his friend.

27. Owain (โอเว่น - a <u>fish</u>) stops to talk to Elmo.

28. A <u>bee</u> flies overhead, looking for the party.

29. He sees the party on a floating <u>lid</u>.

30. More bees arrive carrying food and drink on <u>trays</u>.

31. One big fat bee with a very sweet <u>tooth</u>.

32. <u>Yacht</u> sails by almost upsetting the party.

33. A tired <u>horse</u>, Apache (อาปาชี), is dreaming.

34. Apache dreams of a <u>giant</u> coming to aid him.

35. Then it's back to reality and Apache continues to pull the <u>boat</u> up the river.

36. Moxie (มกชี - a <u>monkey</u>) is looking down from the trees and sees something shiny on the floor.

37. He picks up the shiny <u>ring</u> and wants to return it to its owner.

38. Moxie goes to see the hermit at the <u>tent</u>.

39. Moxie and the <u>hermit</u> talk.

40. Qilin (ขิลิน - the <u>tiger</u>) arrives with a sore head.

41. The hermit looks into the <u>chest</u> to give them gifts.

42. He gives a <u>kite</u> to Moxie (to thank him for being honest).

43. ...and a <u>bowl</u> to Qilin, to steam away his fever.

44. As the sun sets, Jawhar (จอฮาร์ - the <u>owl</u>) watches from the trees.

Bangkok, Paragon at Dusk

Appendix C. Other Language Notes

Here are some other features and aspects of Thai that you need to be aware of and understand.

Appendix C.1 Special Signs and Features

Additional signs that you will see in written Thai:

- The sign ๆ (ไม้ ย-มก) - this is called **Mái Yá-mók** and it means that the previous word needs to be repeated, e.g. จริง ๆ (jing jing - meaning *real, true* or, in this case, *real real* or, *really?*).

Note: this word is pronounced /jing/ and not /jring/ as Rɔɔ Ruua is silent here.

- The sign ฯ **Bpee-yaan-nɔ́ɔi** (เป-ยาล-น้อย) is used for abbreviation, e.g. กรุง-เทพ ฯ - *Grung-têep* (Bangkok).

  When you see this sign you have to pronounce the full word when speaking (if you know it). The full word for Bangkok is *Grung-têep-má-hǎa-ná-kɔɔn* (กรุง-เทพ-ม-หา-น-คร).

- The sign ฯลฯ (เป-ยาล-ใหญ่) **Bpee-yaan-yài** is used in a similar manner to 'etc.' in English. When spoken, it is pronounced as /lá/ (ละ).

- The sign ์ (กา-รันต์) is called the **gaa-ran** and is used to make the letter it is above silent. It is most commonly seen in western words written in Thai.

  For example, the word beer - biia (เบียร์).

Appendix C.2 Sà-rà Ai Mái-Múuan (ใ-)

Only 20 words in the Thai language use sà-rà ai mái-múuan (ใ- /ai/), these are:

- ใช่ (châi - *yes*)
- ใคร (krai - *who*)
- ใส (săi - *clear*)
- ใบ (bai - *leaf*)
- ใจ (jai - *heart*)
- ใต้ (dtâi - *south, underneath*)
- ใฝ่ (fài - *aim*)
- ให้ (hâi - *give, let, permit*)
- ใหญ่ (yài - *big, large*)
- ใหม่ (mài - *new, again*)

- ใช้ (chái - *use*)
- ใคร่ (krâi - *desire*)
- ใส่ (sài - *put in*)
- ใบ้ (bâi - *mute, dumb*)
- ใด (dai - *any*)
- ใน (nai - *in*)
- ใย (yai - *web, fiber*)
- ใกล้ (glâi - *near, close*)
- สะใภ้ (sà-pái - *daughter in law*)
- หลง-ใหล (lŏng-lăi - *fascinating*)

Appendix C.3 Double ร (ร หัน - Rɔɔ Hăn)

- You will sometimes see a double cluster of Rɔɔ Rʉʉa (รร) when reading Thai. This is called *Rɔɔ Hăn* (ร หัน) and is either pronounced as /a/ when it is in the medial position in a syllable or as /an/ when in the final position. For example:

- มรรค (mák - *path*)

- สรรพ (sàp - *whole, all, entire*)

- สรร (săn - *choose*)

- บรรจุ (ban-jù - *load, fill*).

Appendix C.4 Consonant Clusters

Consonant clusters are groups of two consonants at the beginning of a syllable. Here are the five initial consonant sounds:

Table C.4.1 - Initial Consonants

Initial Consonant(s)	Sound
ก	**/g/**
ข and ค	**/k/**
ต	**/dt/**
ป	**/bp/**
ผ and พ	**/p/**

The second consonant will always be either ร (Rɔɔ Rʉʉa), ล (Lɔɔ Ling) or ว (Wɔɔ Wɛ̌ɛn).

The following table shows the complete list of consonant clusters:

Table C.4.2 - List of Consonant Clusters

Cluster	Pronuncia-tion	Example
กร-	/gr/	โกรธ (gròot - *angry*)
กล-	/gl/	กลับ (glàp - *return, go back*)
กว-	/gw/	กว่า (gwàa - *more*)
ขร-	/kr/	ขรึม (krʉm - *serious*)
ขล-	/kl/	ขลุ่ย (klùi - *flute*)
ขว-	/kw/	ขวา (kwǎa - *right*)
คร-	/kr/	ครับ (kráp - *polite particle used by males*)
คล-	/kl/	โคลง (kloong - *poem, poetry*)
คว-	/kw/	ความ (kwaam - *a prefix that converts a verb or an adjective into an abstract noun*)
ตร-	/dtr/	ตรง (dtrong - *at, straight*)
ปร-	/bpr/	ประ-เทศ (bprà-têet - *country, nation*)
ปล-	/bpl/	ปลา (bplaa - *fish*)

Table C.4.2 - List of Consonant Clusters

Cluster	Pronunciation	Example
ผล-	/pl/	ผลัก (plàk - *push, shove*)
พร-	/pr/	พระ (prá - *buddha image or statue*)
พล-	/pl/	พลิก (plík - *turn over*)

Appendix C.5 Tɔɔ & Rɔɔ

Tɔɔ Tá-hǎan (ท) does not form a consonant cluster. However, when the second consonant is *Rɔɔ Rʉʉa* (ร) there are seventeen instances in Thai language where they form a separate sound of **sɔɔ** (/s/); this is from the consonant *sɔɔ sôo* (ซ).

This amalgamation can be written as: ท+ร = ซ or /t/+/r/ = /s/.

This may appear confusing but try and remember **Tɔɔ + Rɔɔ = Sɔɔ**

These words are:

- ทรวด-ทรง (sûuat-song - *shape, contour*)
- ทราม (saam - *low, inferior*)
- ทรุด (sút - *sink*)
- อิน-ทรี (in-sii - *eagle*)
- มั้-ทรี (Mát-sii - *girl's name*)
- นน-ทรี (non-sii - *type of tree*)
- ทรวง (suuang - *chest, breast*)
- ทรัพย์ (sáp - *wealth, property, estate*)
- ฉะ-เชิง-เทรา (Chà-chəəng-sao - *Thai province*)

- ทราบ (sâap - *know (formal)*)
- ทราย (saai - *sand*)
- โทรม (soom - *shabby, worn out*)
- อิน-ทรีย์ (in-sii - *organic, organic fertiliser*)
- เทริด (sə̂ət - *crown*)
- พุ-ทรา (pút-saa - *type of fruit*)
- ไทร (sai - *Banyan Tree*)
- แทรก (sɛ̂ɛk - *insert*)

Appendix C.6 Classifiers for Nouns

One helpful aspect of learning Thai is that nouns are only ever singular and, unlike English, they do not need to be changed if or when they become plural. i.e. '*man*' does not become '*men*' in Thai, '*box*' does not become '*boxes*'.

This means you don't have to learn singular/plural forms but you need to learn the noun form classifiers to be able to correctly express quantities of nouns.

Appendix C.6.1 How Are Classifiers Used?

Where **no adjective** is present, the word order is normally:

noun + number + classifier

e.g. năng-sǔu-pim + sɔ̌ɔng + chà-bap

newspaper + two + copies

(หนัง-สือ-พิมพ์ + สอง + ฉ-บับ)

As a sentence this could be:

"*Chăn ao năng-sǔu-pim sɔ̌ɔng chà-bap kâ.*"

(ฉัน เอา หนัง-สือ-พิมพ์ สอง ฉ-บับ ค่ะ)

"*I want two newspapers.*"

Where there is an adjective present, the order within the phrase is most often:

noun + adjective + number + classifier

e.g. biia + yài + nùng + kùat

beer + large + one + bottle

(เบียร์ + ใหญ่ + หนึ่ง + ขวด)

As a sentence:

"*Pŏm ao biia yài nùng kùat kráp.*"

(ผม เอา เบียร์ ใหญ่ หนึ่ง ขวด ครับ)

"*I would like a large bottle of beer please.*"

Note: In these examples we are illustrating how the sentence is structured and spoken in everyday Thai.

Appendix C.6.2 Common Classifiers

There are literally hundreds of classifiers in Thai language, here are some of the common ones:

- baan (บาน) for windows, doors, picture frames, mirrors, e.g. ประตู 2 บาน (*bprà-dtoo sɔ̌ɔng baan - 2 doors*)

- chà-bàp (ฉ-บับ) for letters, newspapers, e.g. จด-หมาย 3 ฉ-บับ (*jòt-mǎai saam chà-bàp - 3 letters*)

- gɛ́ɛo (แก้ว) for drinking glasses, tumblers e.g. *Could I have a glass of beer please?* - pǒm kɔ̌ɔ biia nùng gɛ́ɛo kráp (ผม ขอ เบียร์ หนึ่ง แก้ว ครับ)

- bai (ใบ) for empty glasses, e.g. *Could I have a glass please?* - chǎn kɔ̌ɔ gɛ́ɛo nùng bai kâ (ฉัน ขอ แก้ว หนึ่ง ใบ ค่ะ)

- dtôn (ต้น) for trees, plants, posts

- dtuua (ตัว) for animals, insects, fish, tables and chairs, shirts, pants, coats, other living creatures

- duuang (ดวง) for stars, postage stamps

- fɔɔng (ฟอง) for poultry eggs

- glàk (กลัก) for matchboxes

- gɔ̂ɔn (ก้อน) for lumps of sugar, stones

- hɔ̀ɔ (ห่อ) for bundles, parcels

- kon (คน) for a person, a child, human beings

- kûu (คู่) for pairs of articles, e.g. husband and wife, fork and spoon, etc.

- krûuang (เครื่อง) for electrical appliances: TVs, computers, phones, stereos, etc.

- lêem (เล่ม) for books, candles, scissors

- lam (ลำ) for boats, ships, aeroplanes

- mét (เม็ด) for smaller things, fruit pits, pills

- muan (มวน) for cigarettes

- pὲεn (แผ่น) for sheets of paper, planks of wood

- ong (องค์) for holy personages, kings, and monks

- rɯɯan (เรือน) for clocks, watches

- rûup (รูป) for monks and novices, also for pictures

- sǎai (สาย) for roads, waterways, belts, etc

- sɔ̌ɔng (ซอง) for envelopes

- tûai (ถ้วย) for ceramic cups

- an (อัน) for small objects, things (in general)

- wong (วง) for rings, bracelets, a circle.

Appendix D. Writing Vowels and Other Characters

The following sections show you how to write all the Thai vowels and other language signs. Understanding the correct height of the vowels is important so we include two dashed lines to show the approximate base and height of the consonant.

Appendix D.1 Vowels

Remember, where possible, always start with the loop.

Vowels Before the Consonant

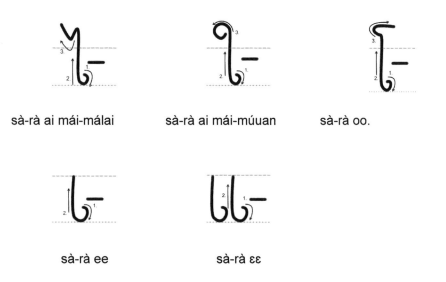

sà-rà ai mái-málai   sà-rà ai mái-múuan   sà-rà oo.

sà-rà ee   sà-rà εε

Vowels After the Consonant

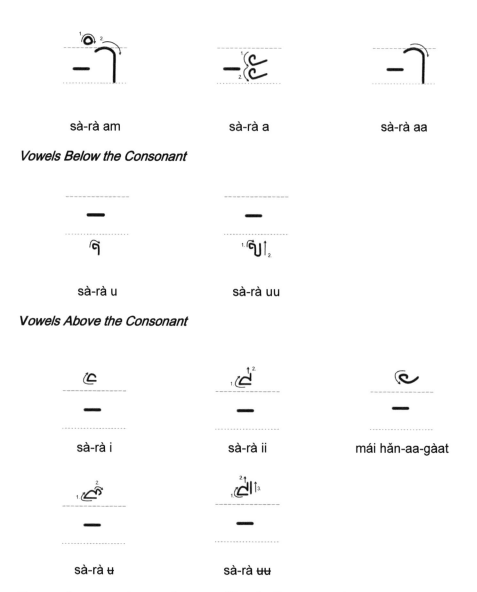

| sà-rà am | sà-rà a | sà-rà aa |

Vowels Below the Consonant

| sà-rà u | sà-rà uu |

Vowels Above the Consonant

| sà-rà i | sà-rà ii | mái hǎn-aa-gàat |

| sà-rà ʉ | sà-rà ʉʉ |

Remember, vowels are always written in the same place
and if you are writing a complex vowel such as the
tripthong sà-rà เ–ือ (/ʉʉa/) then this is comprised of three
individual vowels as shown:

Appendix E. Numbers, Counting and Time

This section explains numbers, counting in Thai, and how to tell the time. However, before we can discuss the time we need to be familiar with numbers.

Appendix E.1 Numbers

Below is the full list of numbers 1 to 99 and then the important numbers above that, 100, 1,000, 10,000, etc.

You will see that *one* is pronounced nὺng, yet 11, 21, and so on, use the suffix -èt (-เอ็ด)

Appendix E.2 Counting

The difference between counting in English and counting in Thai is that you have to be specific about each group of numbers.

For example, with the number 2,367,458, we would say, "Two million, three hundred and sixty-seven thousand, four hundred and fifty-eight."

However, in Thai, you would say, "Two million, three hundred thousand, sixty thousand, seven thousand, four hundred, fifty-eight."

Or actually in [transliterated] Thai:

"sɔ̌ɔng-láan sǎam-sɛ̌ɛn hòk-mὺὺn jèt-pan sìi-rɔ́ɔi hâa-sìp-bpὲɛt (สอง-ล้าน สาม-แสน หก-หมื่น เจ็ด-พัน สี่-ร้อย ห้า-สิบ-แปด).

This is, of course, ๒,๓๖๗,๔๕๘ in Thai numerals.

0 - ๐ - sǔun (ศูนย์)

1 - ๑ - nὲng (หนึ่ง)

2 - ๒ - sɔ̌ɔng (สอง)

3 - ๓ - sǎam (สาม)

4 - ๔ - sìi (สี่)

5 - ๕ - hâa (ห้า)

6 - ๖ - hòk (หก)

7 - ๗ - jèt (เจ็ด)

8 - ๘ - bpὲὲt (แปด)

9 - ๙ - gâo (เก้า)

10 - ๑๐ - sìp (สิบ)

11 - sìp-èt (สิบ-เอ็ด)

12 - sìp-sɔ̌ɔng (สิบ-สอง)

13 - sìp-sǎam (สิบ-สาม)

14 - sìp-sìi (สิบ-สี่)

15 - sìp-hâa (สิบ-ห้า)

16 - sìp-hòk (สิบ-หก)

17 - sìp-jèt (สิบ-เจ็ด)

18 - sìp-bpὲὲt (สิบ-แปด)

19 - sìp-gâo (สิบ-เก้า)

20 - yîi-sìp (ยี่-สิบ)

21- yîi-sìp-èt (ยี่-สิบ-เอ็ด)

22- yîi-sìp-sɔ̌ɔng (ยี่-สิบ-สอง)

23 - yîi-sìp-sǎam (ยี่-สิบ-สาม)

24 - yîi-sìp-sìi (ยี่-สิบ-สี่)

25 - yîi-sìp-hâa (ยี่-สิบ-ห้า)

26 - yîi-sìp-hòk (ยี่-สิบ-หก)

27 - yîi-sìp-jèt (ยี่-สิบ-เจ็ด)

28 - yîi-sìp-bpὲὲt (ยี่-สิบ-แปด)

29 - yîi-sìp-gâo (ยี่-สิบ-เก้า)

30 - sǎam-sìp (สาม-สิบ)

31 - sǎam-sìp-èt (สาม-สิบ-เอ็ด)

32 - sǎam-sìp-sɔ̌ɔng (สาม-สิบ-สอง)

33 - sǎam-sìp-sǎam (สาม-สิบ-สาม)

34 - sǎam-sìp-sìi (สาม-สิบ-สี่)

35 - sǎam-sìp-hâa (สาม-สิบ-ห้า)

36 - sǎam-sìp-hòk (สาม-สิบ-หก)

37 - sǎam-sìp-jèt (สาม-สิบ-เจ็ด)

38 - sǎam-sìp-bpὲὲt (สาม-สิบ-แปด)

39 - sǎam-sìp-gâo (สาม-สิบ-เก้า)

40 - sìi-sìp (สี่-สิบ)

41 - sìi-sìp-èt (สี่-สิบ-เอ็ด)

42 - sìi-sìp-sɔ̌ɔng (สี่-สิบ-สอง)

43 - sìi-sìp-sǎam (สี่-สิบ-สาม)

44 - sìi-sìp-sìi (สี่-สิบ-สี่)

45 - sìi-sìp-hâa (สี่-สิบ-ห้า)

46 - sìi-sìp-hòk (สี่-สิบ-หก)

47 - sìi-sìp-jèt (สี่-สิบ-เจ็ด)

48 - sìi-sìp-bpὲὲt (สี่-สิบ-แปด)

49 - sìi-sìp-gâo (สี่-สิบ-เก้า)

50 - hâa-sìp (ห้า-สิบ)

51 - hâa-sìp-èt (ห้า-สิบ-เอ็ด)

52 - hâa-sìp-sɔ̌ɔng (ห้า-สิบ-สอง)

53 - hâa-sìp-sǎam (ห้า-สิบ-สาม)

54 - hâa-sìp-sìi (ห้า-สิบ-สี่)

55 - hâa-sìp-hâa (ห้า-สิบ-ห้า)

56 - hâa-sìp-hòk (ห้า-สิบ-หก)

57 - hâa-sìp-jèt (ห้า-สิบ-เจ็ด)

58 - hâa-sìp-bpὲὲt (ห้า-สิบ-แปด)

59 - hâa-sìp-gâo (ห้า-สิบ-เก้า)

60 - hòk-sìp (หก-สิบ)

61 - hòk-sìp-èt (หก-สิบ-เอ็ด)

62 - hòk-sìp-sɔ̌ɔng (หก-สิบ-สอง)

63 - hòk-sìp-sǎam (หก-สิบ-สาม)

64 - hòk-sìp-sìi (หก-สิบ-สี่)

65 - hòk-sìp-hâa (หก-สิบ-ห้า)

66 - hòk-sìp-hòk (หก-สิบ-หก)

67 - hòk-sìp-jèt (หก-สิบ-เจ็ด)

68 - hòk-sìp-bpὲὲt (หก-สิบ-แปด)

69 - hòk-sìp-gâo (หก-สิบ-เก้า)

70 - jèt-sìp (เจ็ด-สิบ)

71 - jèt-sìp-èt (เจ็ด-สิบ-เอ็ด)

72 - jèt-sìp-sɔ̌ɔng (เจ็ด-สิบ-สอง)

73 - jèt-sìp-sǎam (เจ็ด-สิบ-สาม)

74 - jèt-sìp-sìi (เจ็ด-สิบ-สี่)

75 - jèt-sìp-hâa (เจ็ด-สิบ-ห้า)

76 - jèt-sìp-hòk (เจ็ด-สิบ-หก)

77 - jèt-sìp-jèt (เจ็ด-สิบ-เจ็ด)

78 - jèt-sìp-bpὲὲt (เจ็ด-สิบ-แปด)

79 - jèt-sìp-gâo (เจ็ด-สิบ-เก้า)

80 - bpὲὲt -sìp (แปด-สิบ)

81 - bpὲὲt-sìp-èt (แปด-สิบ-เอ็ด)

82 - bpὲὲt-sìp-sɔ̌ɔng (แปด-สิบ-สอง)

83 - bpὲὲt-sìp-sǎam (แปด-สิบ-สาม)

84 - bpὲὲt-sìp-sìi (แปด-สิบ-สี่)

85 - bpὲὲt-sìp-hâa (แปด-สิบ-ห้า)

86 - bpὲὲt-sìp-hòk (แปด-สิบ-หก)

87 - bpὲὲt-sìp-jèt (แปด-สิบ-เจ็ด)

88 - bpὲὲt-sìp-bpὲὲt (แปด-สิบ-แปด)

89 - bpὲὲt-sìp-gâo (แปด-สิบ-เก้า)

90 - gâo-sìp (เก้า-สิบ)

91 - gâo-sìp-èt (เก้า-สิบ-เอ็ด)

92 - gâo-sìp-sɔ̌ɔng (เก้า-สิบ-สอง)

93 - gâo-sìp-sǎam (เก้า-สิบ-สาม)

94 - gâo-sìp-sìi (เก้า-สิบ-สี่)

95 - gâo-sìp-hâa (เก้า-สิบ-ห้า)

96 - gâo-sìp-hòk (เก้า-สิบ-หก)

97 - gâo-sìp-jèt (เก้า-สิบ-เจ็ด)

98 - gâo-sìp-bpὲὲt (เก้า-สิบ-แปด)

99 - gâo-sìp-gâo (เก้า-สิบ-เก้า)

100 - nɰ̀ng-rɔ́ɔi (หนึ่ง-ร้อย)

101 - nɰ̀ng-rɔ́ɔi-èt (หนึ่ง-ร้อย-เอ็ด)

111 - nɰ̀ng-rɔ́ɔi sìp-èt (หนึ่ง-ร้อย สิบ-เอ็ด)

300 - sǎam-rɔ́ɔi (สาม-ร้อย)

900 - gâo-rɔ́ɔi (เก้า-ร้อย)

1000 - nɰ̀ng-pan (หนึ่ง-พัน)

10,000 - nɰ̀ng-mɰ̀ɰn (หนึ่ง-หมื่น)

100,000 - nɰ̀ng-sɛ̌ɛn (หนึ่ง-แสน)

1,000,000 - nɰ̀ng-láan (หนึ่ง-ล้าน)

Appendix E.3 Time

Two methods of time are used in Thailand: the first is the 24-hour clock and is used to some extent in bus stations, train stations, government buildings, airports, etc.; but, elsewhere a totally different system is used.

This second system is where the day is broken down into 4 periods of 5 or 6 hours each and each period is referred to differently.

0100 to 0500 - the hour is preceeded by dtii (ตี):

Informal (Speaking)	Formal
1 am - dtii nùng (ตี หนึ่ง)	nùng naa-lí-gaa (หนึ่ง นา-ฬิ-กา)
2 am - dtii sɔ̌ɔng (ตี สอง)	sɔ̌ɔng naa-lí-gaa (สอง นา-ฬิ-กา)
3 am - dtii sǎam (ตี สาม)	sǎam naa-lí-gaa (สาม นา-ฬิ-กา)
4 am - dtii sìi (ตี สี่)	sìi naa-lí-gaa (สี่ นา-ฬิ-กา)
5 am - dtii hâa (ตี ห้า)	hâa naa-lí-gaa (ห้า นา-ฬิ-กา)

- Dtrong (ตรง) means *straight* and refers to the exact hour.

0600 to 1100 - the hour is followed by moong cháo (โมง เช้า):

Informal (Speaking)	Formal
6 am - hòk moong cháo (หก โมง เช้า)	hòk naa-lí-gaa (หก นา-ฬิ-กา)
7 am - jèt moong cháo (เจ็ด โมง (เช้า))	jèt naa-lí-gaa (เจ็ด นา-ฬิ-กา)
8 am - bpɛ̀ɛt moong cháo (แปด โมง (เช้า))	bpɛ̀ɛt naa-lí-gaa (แปด นา-ฬิ-กา)
9 am - gâo moong cháo (เก้า โมง (เช้า))	gâo naa-lí-gaa (เก้า นา-ฬิ-กา)
10 am - sìp moong cháo (สิบ โมง (เช้า))	sìp naa-lí-gaa (สิบ นา-ฬิ-กา)
11 am - sìp-èt moong cháo (สิบ-เอ็ด โมง (เช้า))	sìp-èt naa-lí-gaa (สิบ-เอ็ด นา-ฬิ-กา)
Midday - tîiang dtrong (เที่ยง ตรง)	sìp-sɔ̌ɔng naa-lí-gaa (สิบ-สอง นา-ฬิ-กา)

1300 to 1500 - the hour is preceeded by bàai (บ่าย), meaning early afternoon:

Informal (Speaking)	Formal
1 pm - bàai (nùng) moong (บ่าย (หนึ่ง) โมง)	sìp-săam naa-lí-gaa (สิบ-สาม นา-ฬิ-กา)
2 pm - bàai sɔ̌ɔng (moong) (บ่าย สอง (โมง))	sìp-sìi naa-lí-gaa (สิบ-สี่ นา-ฬิ-กา)
3 pm - bàai săam (moong) (บ่าย สาม (โมง))	sìp-hâa naa-lí-gaa (สิบ-ห้า นา-ฬิ-กา)

1600 to 1800 - the hour is followed by yen (เย็น), meaning late afternoon:

Informal (Speaking)	Formal
4 pm - sìi moong yen (สี่ โมง เย็น)	sìp-hòk naa-lí-gaa (สิบ-หก นา-ฬิ-กา)
5 pm - hâa moong yen (ห้า โมง เย็น)	sìp-jèt naa-lí-gaa (สิบ-เจ็ด นา-ฬิ-กา)
6 pm - hòk moong yen (หก โมง เย็น)	sìp-bpὲὲt naa-lí-gaa (สิบ-แปด นา-ฬิ-กา)

1900 to 2300 - the hour is followed by tûm (ทุ่ม):

Informal (Speaking)	Formal
7 pm - nùng tûm (หนึ่ง ทุ่ม)	sìp-gâo naa-lí-gaa (สิบ-เก้า นา-ฬิ-กา)
8 pm - sɔ̌ɔng tûm (สอง ทุ่ม)	yîi-sìp naa-lí-gaa (ยี่-สิบ นา-ฬิ-กา)
9 pm - săam tûm (สาม ทุ่ม)	yîi-sìp-èt naa-lí-gaa (ยี่-สิบ-เอ็ด นา-ฬิ-กา)
10 pm - sìi tûm (สี่ ทุ่ม)	yîi-sìp-sɔ̌ɔng naa-lí-gaa (ยี่-สิบ-สอง นา-ฬิ-กา)
11 pm - hâa tûm (ห้า ทุ่ม)	yîi-sìp-săam naa-lí-gaa (ยี่-สิบ-สาม นา-ฬิ-กา)
Midnight - tîiang kʉʉn (เที่ยง คืน)	yîi-sìp-sìi naa-lí-gaa (ยี่-สิบ-สี่ นา-ฬิ-กา)

Note: You may hear midnight being referred to as hòk tûm (หก ทุ่ม), but it is rarely used.

Appendix E.3.1 Confusion?

Early Mornings

There can occasionally be some confusion when referring to time in the second period of the day, 0600 - 1100 (or more precisely, from 0700). Though this method of telling the time is not used as much nowadays, it can still be referred to.

Time can be referred to in two ways: as we have written above, i.e. 6 am - hòk moong cháo (หก โมง เช้า), 7 am - jèt moong cháo (เจ็ด โมง เช้า), etc. or it can be referred to as the, '1st hour of the morning', the '2nd hour of the morning', etc.

- 6 am - *hòk moong cháo* (หก โมง เช้า) - sixth hour morning
- 7 am - *nùng moong cháo* (หนึ่ง โมง เช้า) - 1st hour morning
- 8 am - *sǒɔng moong cháo* (สอง โมง เช้า) - 2nd hour morning
- 9 am - *sǎam moong cháo* (สาม โมง เช้า) - 3rd hour morning
- 10 am - *sìi moong cháo* (สี่ โมง เช้า) - 4th hour morning
- 11 am - *hâa moong cháo* (ห้า โมง เช้า) - 5th hour morning

Here you can see where confusion could arise: 6 am, which is always referred to as *hòk moong cháo* (หก โมง เช้า), is the *6th hour of the morning,* yet 7 am, which comes after 6 am, is referred to as the*1st hour of the morning.*

Personally, and it helps being ex-military, Russ prefers to refer to the 7th and subsequent hours as เจ็ด โมง เช้า, แปด โมง เช้า, etc., as it avoids any confusion.

Good Afternoon

Some also say that 4pm in our afternoon transition period should be classed as *bàai sìi moong* (บ่าย สี่ โมง) and not as written, *sìi moong yen* (สี่ โมง เย็น): it all depends on your definition of 'late afternoon'.

Appendix F. Useful Phrases

Here are some more useful, basic conversational phrases to help you in the Land of Smiles. Don't forget to use kâ or kráp (as appropriate) and always remember, wherever you are, a smile goes a long way!

Appendix F.1 Basic Conversation

- Yes - *châi* (ใช่) or *kráp* (ครับ) or *kâ* (ค่ะ): *kráp/kâ* can also be used to indicate agreement.

- No - *mâi* (ไม่)

- Thank you - *kɔ̀ɔp-kun* (ขอบ-คุณ)

- Hello - *sà-wàt-dii* (ส-วัส-ดี)

- How are you/are you well? - *kun sà-baai dii mǎi* (คุณ ส-บาย ดี ไหม)

- I'm fine/I'm well - *pǒm sà-baai dii* (ผม ส-บาย ดี)

- Not well - *mâi sà-baai* (ไม่ ส-บาย)

- Good luck - *chôok dii* (โชค ดี)

- Please - *gà-rú-naa* (ก-รุ-ณา)

Appendix F.2 About Yourself

- My name is... (male) - *pǒm chûu...* (ผม ชื่อ...)

- My name is .... (female) - *dì-chǎn chûu...* (ดิ-ฉัน ชื่อ ...)

- What's your name? - *kun chûu à-rai* (คุณ ชื่อ อะ-ไร)

- His/her name is... - *kǎo chûu..*(เขา ชื่อ...)

- How old are you? - *kun aa-yú tâo rai* (คุณ อา-ยุ เท่า ไร)

- I am 30 years old - *pǒm aa-yú sǎam-sìp bpii* (ผม อา-ยุ สาม-สิบ ปี)

Appendix F.3 Asking Questions

- Where? - *tîi-nǎi* (ที่-ไหน), e.g. Where is the toilet? - *hɔ̂ɔng nám yùu tîi-nǎi* (ห้อง น้ำ อยู่ ที่-ไหน)

- Who? - *krai* (ใคร), e.g. Who is that? - *nân kuu krai* (นั่น คือ ใคร)

- Whose? - *kɔ̌ɔng krai* (ของ ใคร), e.g. Whose pen is that? - *nân kʉʉ bpàak-gaa kɔ̌ɔng krai* (นั่น คือ ปาก-กา ของ ใคร)

- Why? - *tam-mai* (ทำ-ไม), e.g. Why did you say that? - *tam-mai kun pûut bὲɛp nán* (ทำ-ไม คุณ พูด แบบ นั่น)

- What? - *à-rai* (อะ-ไร), e.g. What is the time? - *wee-laa à-rai lέɛo* (เว-ลา อะ-ไร แล้ว) or you can use *gìi moong lέɛo* (กี่ โมง แล้ว)

- When? - *mʉ̂ʉa-rai* (เมื่อ-ไร), e.g. When does the shop open? - *ráan bpɤ̀ɤt mʉ̂ʉa-rài* (ร้าน เปิด เมื่อ-ไร)

- Please speak slowly - *gà-rú-naa pûut cháa cháa nɔ̀ɔi* (ก-รุ-ณา พูด ช้าๆ หน่อย)

- Can you speak English? - *kun pûut paa-sǎa ang-grìt dâi mǎi* (คุณ พูด ภา-ษา อัง-กฤษ ได้ ไหม)

- What's that? - *nân kʉʉ à-rai* (นั่น คือ อะไร)

- Please repeat that - *gà-rú-naa pûut ìik tii* (ก-รุ-ณา พูด อีก ที)

Appendix F.4 Other Useful Expressions and Phrases

- Excuse me - *kɔ̌ɔ-tôot* (ขอ-โทษ)

- Sorry (apology) - *kɔ̌ɔ-tôot* (ขอ-โทษ)

- Sorry (feeling regret) - *sǐia-jai* (เสีย-ใจ)

- I don't speak Thai - *pǒm pûut tai mâi dâi* (ผม พูด ไทย ไม่ ได้)

- I already have one - *chǎn mii lέɛo* (ฉัน มี แล้ว)

- I don't have one - *pǒm mâi mii* (ผม ไม่ มี)

- I don't have one now - *chǎn mâi mii lέɛo* (ฉัน ไม่ มี แล้ว)

- I'm sorry, I don't understand - *kɔ̌ɔ-tôot kráp pǒm mâi kâo-jai* (ขอ-โทษ ครับ ผม ไม่ เข้า-ใจ)

- No, thank you, I don't want it - *chǎn mâi ao kâ kɔ̀ɔp-kun kâ* (ฉัน ไม่ เอา ค่ะ ขอบ-คุณ ค่ะ)

Appendix G. Lists

The next few pages details lists of items that will help expand your vocabulary and include such items as *Personal Pronouns, Verbs, Nouns, Adjectives, Cooking Terms*, etc.

Appendix G.1 Personal Pronouns

The following is the list of most common personal pronouns. There are more but just learning these will see you well on your way to conversing effectively in Thai.

- *I, me* - pǒm (ผม) (formal) is a polite word used only by males.

- *I, me* - dì-chǎn (ดิ-ฉัน) (formal) is a polite word used only by females.

- *I, me* - chǎn (ฉัน) (informal)

  ฉัน is another personal pronoun that is used by both men and women; it is not something that you hear in day-to-day use. It is a word that is used amongst intimates, with very close friends, or when you are talking to people of a lower social rank than you, i.e. servants.
  Never use it with people of a higher rank or social status than yourself.

- *You* - təə (เธอ)

  เธอ is another very familiar form of address. It is used mainly by women talking to each other. It is often used in conjunction with chǎn (above).

- *You* - kun (คุณ) is a polite word used by males and females. This is the word most commonly heard in daily conversation.

- *He, she* - kǎo (เขา) is used by either sex referring to just about anyone.

- *You, he, she* - tâan (ท่าน) is used when talking or referring to a person of higher rank than yourself, e.g. to monks, to the Prime Minister, etc.

- *They* - pûuak kǎo (พวก-เขา)

- *We, us* - pûuak rao (พวก-เรา)

Appendix G.2 Verbs

- *Ask* - tâam (ถาม)

- *Bite* - gàt (กัด)

- *Brush* - bprɛɛng (แปรง)

- *Climb* - bpiin (ปีน)

- *Come* - maa (มา)

- *Cook* - tam aa-hǎan (ทำ อา-หาร)

- *Cry* - rɔ́ɔng-hâi (ร้อง-ไห้)

- *Cut* - dtàt (ตัด)

- *Dance* - dtêen-ram (เต้น-รำ)

- *Do* - tam (ทำ)

- *Drink* - dʉ̀ʉm (ดื่ม)

- *Drive* - kàp (ขับ)

- *Eat* - gin (กิน)

- *Find* - jəə (เจอ)

- *Forget* - lʉʉm (ลืม)

- *Go* - bpai (ไป)

- *Have* - mii (มี)

- *Hear* - dâi-yin (ได้-ยิน)

- *Help* - chûuai (ช่วย)

- *Jump* - grà-dòot (กระ-โดด)

- *Know (something)* - rúu (รู้)

- *Know (someone)* - rúu-jàk (รู้-จัก)

- *Learn* - riian-rúu (เรียน-รู้)

- *Like* - chɔ̂ɔp (ชอบ)

- *Listen* - fang (ฟัง)

- *Look* - duu (ดู)

- *Look for* - mɔɔng-hǎa (มอง-หา)

- *Love* - rák (รัก)

- *Meet* - póp (พบ)

- *Need* - jam-bpen-dtɔ̂ɔng (จำ-เป็น-ต้อง)

- *Play* - lêen (เล่น)

- *Pull* - dʉng (ดึง)

- *Push* - plàk (ผลัก)

- *Put (down)* - waang (วาง)

- *Read* - àan (อ่าน)

- *Remember* - jam (จำ)

- *Ride* - kìi (ขี่)

- *Run* - wîng (วิ่ง)

- *See* - hěn (เห็น)

- *Sing* - rɔ́ɔng-pleeng (ร้อง-เพลง)

- *Sit* - nâng (นั่ง)

- Sleep - nɔɔn (นอน)

- *Stand* - yʉʉn (ยืน)

- *Study* - riian (เรียน)

- *Swim* - wâai (ว่าย)

- *Teach* - sɔ̌ɔn (สอน)

- *Think* - kít (คิด)

- *Understand* - kâo-jai (เข้า-ใจ)

- *Use* - chái (ใช้)

- *Walk* - dəən (เดิน)

- *Want* - dtɔ̂ɔng-gaan (ต้อง-การ)

- *Watch* - fâo-duu (เฝ้า-ดู)

- *Write* - kĭian (เขียน).

Appendix G.3 Adjectives

- *Big* - yài (ใหญ่)

- *Little* - nít-nɔ̀ɔi (นิด-หน่อย)

- *Fast* - réo (เร็ว)

- *Slow* - cháa (ช้า)

- *Happy* - mii kwaam sùk (มี ความ สุข)

- *Sad* - sâo (เศร้า)

- *Long* - yaao (ยาว)

- *Short* - dtîia (เตี้ย)

- *Loud* - dang (ดัง)

- *Quiet* - ngîiap (เงียบ)

- *Tall* - sŭung (สูง)

- *Small* - lék (เล็ก)

- *Angry* - gròot (โกรธ)

- *Difficult, hard* - yâak (ยาก)

- *Warm (friendly)* - òp-ùn (อบ-อุ่น)

- *Friendly* - bpen-mít (เป็น-มิตร)

- *Hostile* - mâi bpen-mít (ไม่ เป็น-มิตร)

- *Hard, heavy* - nàk (หนัก)

- *Easy* - ngâai (ง่าย)

- *Light (weight)* - bao (เบา)

- *Dark* - mûut (มืด)

- *Light (bright)* - sà-wàang (สว่าง)

- *Good* - dii (ดี)

- *Bad* - leeo (เลว)

- *Beautiful* - sŭuai (สวย)

- *Ugly* - nâa-glìat (น่า-เกลียด)

- *Hungry* - hĭo (หิว)

- *Full (up - with food)* - ìm (อิ่ม)

- *Strong* - kĕng-rɛɛng (แข็ง-แรง)

- *Weak* - ɔ̀ɔn-ɛɛ (อ่อน-แอ)

- *Old* - gào (เก่า)

- *Young (adolescent)* - nùm (male), săao (female) (หนุ่ม, สาว)

- *Rich* - ruai (รวย)

- *Poor* - jon (จน)

- *Expensive* - pɛɛng (แพง)

- *Cheap* - tùuk (ถูก).

Appendix G.4 Seasons

Thailand has three seasons (season is called rɯ-duu (ฤ-ดู)), hot, rainy and cold. These are:

- *Hot season* (March to May) - *rɯ-duu rɔ́ɔn* (ฤ-ดู ร้อน)

- *Rainy season* (June to October) - *rɯ-duu fŏn* (ฤ-ดู ฝน)

- *Cold season* (November to February) - *rɯ-duu năao* (ฤ-ดู หนาว).

Appendix G.5 Colours

- _Black_ - sǐi dam (สี ดำ)

- _Blue_ - sǐi fáa (สี ฟ้า)

- _Brown_ - sǐi nám-dtaan (สี น้ำ-ตาล)

- _Gold_ - sǐi tɔɔng (สี ทอง)

- _Gray_ - sǐi tao (สี เทา)

- _Green_ - sǐi kǐiao (สี เขียว)

- _Khaki_ - sǐi gaa-gii (สี กา-กี)

- _Orange_ - sǐi sôm (สี ส้ม)

- _Purple_ - sǐi mûuang (สี ม่วง)

- _Pink_ - sǐi chom-puu (สี ชม-พู)

- _Red_ - sǐi dɛɛng (สี แดง)

- _Silver_ - sǐi ngəən (สี เงิน)

- _White_ - sǐi kǎao (สี ขาว).

Appendix G.6 Food /Cooking Terms

Thai people love food and talking or thinking about food is almost like the English fixation with the weather, it's almost a lifestyle.

The following is just a small sample of the many wonderful dishes and flavours that can be gotten almost anywhere - delicious!

Cooking Terms

- _Boil_ - dtôm (ต้ม)

- _Steam_ - nûng (นึ่ง) (you may also hear it being called dtǔn (ตุ๋น))

- _Deep fried_ - tɔ̂ɔd (ทอด)

- _Toast_ - bpîng (ปิ้ง)

- _Bake_ - òp (อบ)

- _Barbeque, grill, roast_ - yâang (ย่าง)

- _Fry_ - pàt (ผัด).

Appendix G.7 Commenting

- _Delicious_ - à-rɔ̀ɔi (อ-ร่อย)

- _Not delicious_ - mâi à-rɔ̀ɔi (ไม่ อ-ร่อย)

- _Very delicious_ - à-rɔ̂ɔi mâak (อ-ร่อย มาก)

- _Spicy_ - pèt (เผ็ด)

- _Not spicy_ - mâi pèt (ไม่ เผ็ด)

- _Very Spicy_ - pèt mâak (เผ็ด มาก)

- _Sweet_ - wǎan (หวาน)

- _Sour_ - bprîiao (เปรี้ยว)

- _Salty_ - kem (เค็ม)

- _Bitter_ - kǒm (ขม).

Food

- _Rice_ - kâao (ข้าว) or you may see ข้าว สวย (kâao sǔai - cooked rice)

- _Sticky rice_ - kâao nǐiao (ข้าว เหนียว)

- _Chicken_ - gài (ไก่)

- _Pork_ - mǔu (หมู)

- _Beef_ - núua (เนื้อ)

- _Fish_ - bplaa (ปลา)

- *Chilli* - prík (พริก)

- *Mushroom* - hèt (เห็ด)

- *Onion* - hɔ̌ɔm-hǔua-yài (หอม-หัว-ใหญ่).

Dishes

A selection of some of our favourite Thai dishes:

- *Chicken with sweet chillies* - gài pàt prík yùuak (ไก่ ผัด พริก หยวก)

- *Chicken with basil* - gà-prao gài (กะ-เพรา ไก่)

- *Noodles* - gǔuai dtǐiao (ก๋วย เตี๋ยว)

- *Green sweet chicken curry* - gɛɛng kǐiao wǎan gài (แกง เขียว หวาน ไก่)

- *Thai vermicelli* - kà-nǒm jiin (ข-นม จีน)

- *Rice soup* - kâao dtôm (ข้าว ต้ม)

- *Spicy soup with prawn* - dtôm yam gûng (ต้ม ยำ กุ้ง)

- *Spicy soup with chicken* - dtôm yam gài (ต้ม ยำ ไก่)

- *Thai style Noodled* - pàd Thai (ผัด ไทย)

- *Omelette* - kài jiiao (ไข่ เจียว)

- *Papaya salad* - sôm-dtam (ส้ม-ตำ)

- *Minced pork salad* - lâap (ลาบ).

Appendix G.8 Drinks

- *Water* - nám (น้ำ)

- *Orange* - sôm (ส้ม)

- *Orange juice* - nám sôm (น้ำ ส้ม)

- *Grapefruit* - sôm-oo (ส้ม-โอ)

- *Grapefruit juice* - nám sôm-oo (น้ำ ส้ม-โอ)

- *Pineapple* - sàp-bpà-rót (สับ-ปะ-รด)

- *Coffee* - gaa-fɛɛ (กา-แฟ)

- *Tea* – chaa (ชา)

- *Coke* - kóok (โค้ก)

- *Ice* - náam kěng (น้ำ แข็ง)

- *Beer* - biia (เบียร์)

- *Wine* - wai (ไวน์).

Appendix G.9 Occupations

- *"Kun tam-ngaan à-rai kráp"* (คุณ ทำ-งาน อะ-ไร ครับ) - *"You work what?/What work do you do?"*

- *Cook (male)* - pɔ̂ɔ-kruua (พ่อ-ครัว)

- *Cook (female)* - mɛ̂ɛ-kruua (แม่-ครัว)

- *Dentist* - mɔ̌ɔ-fan (หมอ-ฟัน)

- *Doctor* - mɔ̌ɔ (หมอ), pɛ̂ɛt (แพทย์)

- *Electrician* - châang-fai-fáa (ช่าง-ไฟ-ฟ้า)

- *Engineer* - wít-sà-wá-gɔɔn (วิ-ศ-ว-กร)

- *Farmer - chaao-naa* (ชาว-นา)

- *Hairdresser - châang-tam-pŏm* (ช่าง-ทำ-ผม)

- *Lawyer - tá-naai-kwaam* (ท-นาย-ความ)

- *Mechanic - châang-gon* (ช่าง-กล)

- *Nurse - pá-yaa-baan* (พ-ยา-บาล)

- *Pilot - nák-bìn* (นัก-บิน)

- *Policeman - dtam-rùuat* (ตำ-รวจ)

- *Postman - bù-rùt-bprai-sà-nii* (บุ-รุษ-ไปร-ษ-ณีย์)

- *Sailor - gà-laa-sĭi ~~ruua~~* (กะ-ลา-สี เรือ)

- *Secretary - lee-kăa-nú-gaan* (เล-ขา-นุ-การ)

- *Teacher - kruu* (ครู)

- *Businessman - nák-tú-rá-gìt* (นัก-ธุ-ร-กิจ)

- *Business owner - jâo-kŏong tú-rá-gìt* (เจ้า-ของ ธุ-ร-กิจ)

- *Manager - pûu-jàt-gaan* (ผู้-จัด-การ)

- *Student - nák-riian* (นัก-เรียน).

Bibliography

* Robson S. & Changchit P., 2007. *Instant Thai.* Tuttle Publishing, 2007

* Becker BP., 1995. *Thai for Beginners.* Paiboon Publishing, 1995

* Becker BP., 1998. *Thai for Intermediate Learners.* Paiboon Publishing, 1998

* Becker BP. & Pirazzi C., 2009. *Three-way Thai-English Dictionary.* Paiboon Publishing, 2009.

* Jai-Ua B., & Golding M., 2003. *Pocket Thai Dictionary.* Periplus, 2003

* กำชัย ทองหล่อ, 2552. หลักภาษาไทย. อมรการพิมพ์ กทม, 2552

* *Thai2English* - Nectec - http://www.thaienglish.com

* Campbell S., & Shaweevong C., 2006. (Online) *The Fundamentals of the Thai Language.* Available at: http://www.lyndonhill.com (Accessed: 05/04/2010)

* Effective Language Learning. (2013). Language Difficulty Ranking. Retrieved March 6th, 2014, from Effective Language Learning: http://www.effectivelanguagelearning.com/language-guide/language-difficulty

* Muay Thai Fighting, 17/02/2008. *Muay Thai Rules* (Online) Available at http://www.muaythai-fighting.com (Accessed: 10/11/2010)

* Wikepedia.*Culture of Thailand* (Online) Available at http://en.wikipedia.org/wiki/Culture_of_Thailand (Accessed: 17/10/2010)

* Siam Foundation. *What are the Buddhist Precepts?* (Online) Available at http://siamfoundation.org/thailand-faq/index.php?action=artikel&cat=5&id=3&artlang=en (Accessed: 22/10/2010)

* http://www.paknam.com (Accessed online: 9th October 2010)

* http://www.thai-language.com/ (Accessed online: 9th October 2010)

* http://www.siamfoundation.org (Accessed online: 9th October 2010)

* http://www.learningthai.com (Accessed online: 17th August 2010)

* http://www.slice-of-thai.com/ (Accessed online: 17th August 2010)

* http://www.rusiedotton.thai.net (Accessed online: 23rd November 2010)

Notes

Index

I

Lúk (ลึก) - deep 140
Lʉʉm (ลืม) - forget 127, 168

M

Maa (มา) - come 36, 64, 168
Máa (ม้า) - horse 121
Mâak (มาก) - very much, a lot, many 17, 33, 121
Mâat (มาด) - appearance or manner 41
Màat (หมาด) - almost dry 41
Mái
    Mái dtài kúu (̄) (ไม้ไต่คู้) 45
    Mái dtrii (̄) (ไม้ตรี) 29
    Mái èek (-) (ไม้เอก) 29
    Mái hǎn-aa-gàat (̄) (ไม้หันอากาศ) 39, 158
    Mái jàt-dtà-waa (-) (ไม้จัตวา) 29
    Mái too (̄) (ไม้โท) 29
    Mái Yá-mók (ๆ) (ไม้ยมก) - repetition sign 151
Mâi
    Mâi (ไม่) – no, not 37, 121, 165
    Mâi à-rɔ̀ɔi (ไม่อร่อย) - not delicious 170
    Mâi bpen rai (ไม่เป็นไร) - never mind, it'll be okay 90, 124
    Mâi bpen-mít (ไม่เป็นมิตร) - hostile 169
    Mâi châi (ไม่ใช่) - not 88
    Mâi chɔ̂ɔp (ไม่ชอบ) - don't like 80
    Mâi mii (ไม่มี) - not have 92
    Mâi pèt (ไม่เผ็ด) - not spicy 170
    Mâi rúu (ไม่รู้) - don't know 60
    Mâi sà-baai (ไม่สบาย) - not well 165
Mài (ใหม่) - new, again 152
Mák (มรรค) - path 152
Man - pûu-chaai (ผู้ชาย) 70
Man (มัน) - it 120, 132
Manager - pûu-jàt-gaan (ผู้จัดการ) 172
Manner - mâat (มาด) 41
March - mii-naa-kom (มีนาคม) 112
Má-rʉʉn-níi (มะรืนนี้) - after tomorrow 84
Matchboxes (classifier) - glàk (กลัก) 156
Mát-sii (มัทรี) - girl's name 154
May - prút-sà-paa-kom (พฤษภาคม) 112
Maybe, might - àat-jà (อาจจะ) 83
Measure - wât (วัด) 129
Mechanic - châang-gon (ช่างกล) 172
Meditate - kâo chaan (เข้าฌาน) 79
Mêek (เมฆ) - cloud 67
Meet
    Go and meet - bpai póp (ไปพบ) 105
    Meet - póp (พบ) 107, 168
Merit, virtue - bun (บุญ) 15

Mét (เม็ด) - classifier for smaller things, fruit pits, pills 156
Mɛ̂ɛ
    Mɛ̂ɛ (แม่) - mother 64, 70
    Mɛ̂ɛ-kruua (แม่ครัว) - cook (female) 171
Midday - tîiang dtrong (เที่ยงตรง) 162
Midnight - tîiang kʉʉn (เที่ยงคืน) 163
Mii
    Mii (มี) - have 132, 168
    Mii (มี) - to be 24, 26
    Mii kâi (มีไข้) - have a temperature, ill, sick 134
    Mii kwaam sùk (มีความสุข) - happy 169
Miia (เมีย) - wife (informal) 71, 121
Milk - nom (นม) 105
Millie (มิลลี่) - name of the chicken 56, 149
Minced pork salad - lâap (ลาบ) 171
Mind - jai (ใจ) 37
Mine, my - kɔ̌ɔng pǒm/chǎn 27
Monday - wan jan (วันจันทร์) 85
Money - ngəən (เงิน) 69
Monk (young) - neen (เณร) 92
Monkey - ling (ลิง) 126
Months of the Year 112
Mon-ton (มณฑล) – county, precinct, circle 89
Moong (โมง) - hour (daytime), o'clock 37
Moral Precepts 104
More
    More - gwàa (กว่า) 153
    More - ìik (อีก) 37
Morning
    Morning - cháo (เช้า) 43
    Morning - dtɔɔn-cháo (ตอนเช้า) 143
Mòt (หมด) - empty, finish 137
Mother
    Mother - mɛ̂ɛ (แม่) 65, 70
    Mother or father's older brother - lung (ลุง) 72
    Mother or father's older sister - bpâa (ป้า) 72
    Mother's father - dtaa (ตา) 72
    Mother's younger brother or sister - náa (น้า) 72
Mouse - nǔu (หนู) 104
Movie - nǎng (หนัง) 137
Moxie (มกซี่) - name of the monkey 126, 150
Mɔ̌ɔ
    Mɔ̌ɔ (หมอ) - doctor 171
    Mɔ̌ɔ-fan (หมอฟัน) - dentist 171
Mɔɔ Máa (ม ม้า) - 33rd letter of the alphabet 121
Mɔɔng-hǎa (มองหา) - look for 168

With - gàp (กับ) 57
Wít-sà-wá-gɔɔn (วิศวกร) - engineer 171
Woman - pûu-yǐng (ผู้หญิง) 63, 70
Wonder - sǒng-sǎi (สงสัย) 129, 143
Wong (วง) - classifier for rings, bracelets, circles 157
Work - ngaan (งาน) 27
Worn out, shabby - soom (โทรม) 154
Would
    Would - kong jà (คงจะ) 121
    Would like - yàak (อยาก) 44, 83, 133
Wɔɔ Wɛ̌ɛn (ว แหวน) - 37th letter of the alphabet 129
Write - kǐian (เขียน) 169
Writing Transliterated Tones 7
Wrong, incorrect - pìt (ผิด) 111

Y

Yâa (ย่า) - father's mother 71
Yaai (ยาย) - grandmother (mother's mother) 72
Yâak (ยาก) - hard, difficult 44, 123, 169
Yàak (อยาก) - would like 44, 82, 132
Yàang
    Yàang (อย่าง) - as, like 44
    Yàang ngâai (อย่างง่าย) - easily 122
    Yàang-rai (อย่างไร) - how 128
Yâang - grill 44
Yaao (ยาว) - long 32, 169
Yâat (ญาติ) – relations, kin, cousins, etc. 81
Yai (ใย) - web, fiber 152
Yài (ใหญ่) - big, large 152, 169
Yang (ยัง) - yet, still 123
Yawn - hǎao (หาว) 69
Year - bpii (ปี) 61, 73, 109
Yes

Yes - kráp (ครับ) 109
Yes, agree - châi (ใช่) 152
Yesterday - mûua-waan-níi (เมื่อวานนี้) 84
Yet, still - yang (ยัง) 123
Yím (ยิ้ม) - smile 98
Yǐng (หญิง) - woman 81
You
    You (formal) - kun (คุณ) 56
    You (informal) - təə (เธอ) 56, 167
    You, he, she - tâan (ท่าน). Used when talking or referring to someone of a higher status than you, e,g, monks. 167
Young
    Young (adolescent, female) - sǎao (สาว) 169
    Young (adolescent, male) - nùm (หนุ่ม) 169
    Younger brother - nɔ́ɔng-chaai (น้องชาย) 71
Yours - kɔ̌ɔng kun (ของคุณ) 27
Yɔɔ
    Yɔɔ Yák (ย ยักษ์) - 34th letter of the alphabet 123
    Yɔɔ Yǐng (ญ หญิง) - 13th letter of the alphabet 81
Yûng (ยุ่ง) - busy, hectic 104
Yùu
    Yùu (อยู่) - be somewhere, live, stay 23, 60, 126, 141
    Yùu tîi-nǎi (อยู่ที่ไหน) - where is... 68, 106, 110
    Yùu tîi-nân (อยู่ที่นั่น) - ... are there 112
Yʉʉn (ยืน) - stand 168

Z

Zero, 0 - Sǔun (ศูนย์) 131

A Note From the Authors

Duangta and I would like to thank you for placing your trust in us and our Quest system by buying this book **Learning Thai, Your Great Adventure**, and we sincerely hope that it has not only given you a good insight into the Thai language, but also helped show you that Thai isn't as difficult as you perhaps first thought.

Of course, the next step is up to you, but if you bought this book as part of our entire Quest system, we would suggest that you start trying to learn the Thai alphabet with either **Learn Thai Alphabet with Memory Aids to Your Great Adventure**; or, if you have the **Learn Thai Alphabet application**, then with that.

Some customers have written to us and told us how easy it made the entire process for them and, if it has had a similar effect on you, then we'd also like to hear from you.

We stand by our system and what we say and do, and have put enormous time and effort into creating what we feel is **the** best system for learning Thai. At the time of writing, there isn't any other system like it.

Before we go, we would like to request a small favour from you, and that is to ask if you would be so kind as to leave a review on Amazon (or wherever you bought the book) as it's reviews from customers which help others take the leap of faith that you yourself did; and, without assistance from people like you, Indie publishers and new writers like us, will never get off the ground.

Alternatively, if you would like to pen a few words as a testimonial for us to use on the website, in our other products (we are in the process of creating more), then: 1) it will be of great help to us and our potential customers; and 2) we <u>always</u> remember those who have taken the time to help us and our products.

On the next pages are reminders of the other products in Quest and, before we close, we would just like to wish you all the success in your studies and in learning Thai.

Kind regards,

Russ & Duangta (russ@learnthaialphabet.com)

Our Quest Products

The products in *Quest* system are:

Volume I - *Learning Thai, Your Great Adventure* is the place to start your Quest. Introducing the Thai language, the alphabet: the consonants, classes and sounds, vowels, tone, why it's important; and so much more.

Volume II - *Memory Aids to Your Great Adventure* is the book that makes learning the Thai alphabet so simple: it couldn't get any easier.

Volume III - *The Perfect Thai Phrasebook* is for those who not only want an accompaniment on their trip to the Land of Smiles, but is for those who, when they realise (as you did) that they want to learn more about Thailand, its language and its culture, can then use it as an aide-memoir to learning to read Thai: packed with everyday words, phrases, and expressions, that people actually use.

Volume IV - *How to Read Thai* is the book that makes reading Thai not only a reality, but easy. We guide you step-by-step through the process of breaking down Thai sentences into words, and words into syllables. It might sound crazy, but Thai has few spaces and puntuation and the answer to the common questionof , *"Where or how do you start?"* is no longer a mystery.

The Learn Thai Alphabet and Learn Thai Numbers Apps

The Learn Thai Alphabet Application

Some screenshots from the application showing the interface, consonants, consonant classes, vowels, rockstars (hard) level, tone marks, test results, audio, etc.

www.learnthaialphabet.com

Made in the USA
Lexington, KY
16 October 2015